# SPIRITUAL AWAKENINGS

*God has a dream
and the dream comes true
each time one of us awakens.*

BHW

# SPIRITUAL
## AWAKENINGS

### INSIGHTS
### OF THE NEAR-
### DEATH EXPERIENCE
### AND OTHER
### DOORWAYS TO OUR SOUL

## Barbara Harris Whitfield

Foreword by
Charles L. Whitfield, M.D.

**Health Communications, Inc.**
**Deerfield Beach, Florida**

Publisher: Health Communications, Inc.
        3201 S.W. 15th Street
        Deerfield Beach, Florida 33442-8190
*Cover design by Robert Cannata*
*Cover photo © Jim Zuckerman*

This book is dedicated with deep appreciation
and gratitude to

Charles L. Whitfield, M.D.
C. Bruce Greyson, M.D. and
Kenneth Ring, Ph.D.

# Contents

# Contents

# Acknowledgments

Quotes from the writings of Kenneth Ring, Bruce Greyson and Charles L. Whitfield were made possible with their permission. This book is dedicated to them for an infinite number of wonderful reasons. However, the one I will share here is: Without these three men's brilliant work—this book would not have been possible. Thank you, not only from me—but from the countless others who are grateful to you!

My thanks to all who have shared their stories with me. Special appreciation goes to Mary Ellen Layden, Joel Funk, Chuck Darlington, Robynne Moran, Laurie Peters Mirochine, Nancy Clark, Diane Mann, Steven Price, Al Sullivan, Sharon Grant, Joe Geraci, Howard Storm and David Doherty. Special thanks to my clients who allowed me to tell their stories.

My appreciation and gratitude to Gary Seidler, who has believed in this book from its very beginning. Audrey DeLaMartre edited this book from her heart as well as her expertise. Christine E. Belleris and Matthew Diener gave me so many good ideas and guidance. They are responsible for the final form this book has taken.

I want to thank all my children for helping me to "lighten up" throughout the writing of *Spiritual Awakenings*. Finally, my gratitude to the Universe for allowing me to be the messenger of what you are about to read.

# Foreword

Have you had a spiritual awakening? Or do you wonder if you might have had one? A spiritual awakening is an experiential opening to a power greater than ourselves. As a result, we become more aware of and open to our self, others and the Universe. And it is much more, as Barbara Harris describes in detail in this book.

Based on surveys that I have done on people attending my workshops each year, I estimate that at least one in three people have had a spiritual awakening of some sort. Perhaps 25 percent of those spiritual awakenings were triggered by near-death experiences, which is Barbara's emphasis. The remaining 75 percent are triggered by numerous other experiences, from meditation, to childbirth, to "hitting bottom" in a critical or desperate life situation.

Who or what is it that actually does the awakening? Is there a part of us that begins to become more aware and opens to our self, others and the God of our understanding? My sense is that it is our real or True Self that awakens, and not our ego or false self.

## Who Am I? A Map of the Mind

Throughout the struggle of the human condition, many people have asked some important questions: Who am I? What am I doing here? Where am I going? How can I get any peace? While the answers to these questions remain a Divine Mystery, using the healing approach described in this book can help. In beginning to answer these questions, I have found it useful to construct a map of the mind or psyche. And

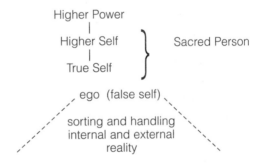

while the map is not the territory, maps can be useful.

Other names for the True Self, who I really am, include the real or existential self, the human heart, the soul and the Child Within.[1] They are all the same because they are our true identity. I also have within me a divine nature, sometimes called a guardian angel, Atman, Buddha Nature, Christ Consciousness, Higher Self or simply Self. And both of these, my True Self and my Higher Self, are intimately connected to my Higher Power, God/Goddess/All-That-Is, a part of which is also within me.

---

[1] See Appendix I for characteristics of the Child Within, or core self.

I see this relationship—True Self, Higher Self and Higher Power—as being such an important relationship that I can also view it as being one Person, which I call the Sacred Person. As a part of the Mystery, my True Self makes or constructs an assistant to help me as I live out this human experience. We can call this assistant, this sidekick, the ego—also known as the false self or co-dependent self. When this ego is helpful to us, such as in screening, sorting and handling many aspects of our internal and external reality, we can call it positive ego. But when it tries to take over and run our life, it becomes negative ego.

This map of the psyche is more evolved than the maps of Freud, Jung and their colleagues of up to 100 years ago, when they used the term "ego" to mean both True Self and false self. Since the 1930s we have begun to make this more precise differentiation between True Self and false self, and today we use "ego" synonymously with false self.

A contemporary holy book called *A Course in Miracles* says in its introduction:

> What is real cannot be threatened.
> What is unreal does not exist.
> Herein lies the peace of God.

What is real is God and God's world, that of the Sacred Person. The ego and its world is not real, and therefore, in the grand scheme of the mystery, does not exist. Herein, when we make this differentiation, lies our peace and serenity.

But growing up in a dysfunctional family and dysfunctional society of origin, we may have become wounded. That wounding made our Child Within, our True Self, go into hiding, and the only one left to run the show of our life was our ego. And since it is not competent to run our life, we often end up feeling confused and hurt.

The way out is to begin to differentiate between identifying with my True Self and my false self, and to heal my

woundedness around all of what happened to hurt and con-
fuse me. That is what I have described in my books.

While all of this information is useful to *know* on a cognitive level, it is *healing* only on an experiential level. To heal,
I have to experience working through my pain as well as living and enjoying my life.

## Spiritual Awakenings and the Recovery Movement

Over the decade of the 1980s and through the 1990s, an
increasing number of people have begun to awaken to many
of their experiences and are beginning to heal themselves.
This phenomenon, called the recovery movement, is part of
a new paradigm, a new and expanded understanding and
belief about the human condition and how to heal it. This
approach is so effective and has developed so much momentum for two reasons: it is *grass roots*—its energy comes from
the recovering people themselves, and it employs the most
accurate and healing of all the accumulated knowledge about
the human condition. But what is different about this knowledge is that it is now *simplified* and *demystified,* and that is
what I believe Barbara Harris has done here with spiritual
awakenings.

## Traps in Spiritual Awakenings

Just as with most things in life, there are some traps in spiritual awakenings. After having had our particular experience,
one trap is being misled by other people who may try to steer
us off of our personal spiritual path. These others may be
therapists, counselors, clergy, gurus, family or friends who
themselves may not understand and may even have distorted
boundaries. And so they may label our awakening as being
psychotic, the work of the devil, hallucinations, flaky; or try
to invalidate our experience in some other way. They may try

to put us on drugs—from sedatives to antidepressants to major tranquilizers. Or lock us up, or shame and guilt us in other ways. But the fact remains that we have had a spiritual awakening, and are looking for validation and support on what really happened and on the rest of our journey.

A second trap is the frustration that usually comes with trying to do what is called a spiritual bypass. A spiritual bypass is when we try to avoid working through the pain of our prior woundedness, so we may try to jump from an earlier stage of healing directly into the most advanced stage. Because this concept is crucial to making sense of and handling spiritual awakenings, I will describe briefly the generic stages of the healing or recovery process.

A spiritual awakening may happen during any of the following stages of recovery.

## Stage Zero

Stage Zero is manifested by the presence of an active illness or disorder, such as an addiction, compulsion or another disorder,

### Recovery and Duration According to Stages

| Recovery Stage | Condition | Focus of Recovery | Approximate Duration |
|---|---|---|---|
| 3 | Human/ Spiritual | Spirituality | Ongoing |
| 2 | Adult Child | Adult-Child Full Recovery Program | 3-5 years |
| 1 | Stage Zero Disorder | Basic-Illness Specific Full Recovery Program | 1/2- 3 yrs |
| 0 | Active Illness | Addiction, Compulsion, Disorder - - - - - - - - Woundedness | Indefinite |

When to focus on Stages 2 and 3 recovery usually depends upon the person's prior healing and present condition.

including any physical illness. This active illness may be acute, recurring or chronic. Without recovery it may continue indefinitely. At Stage Zero, recovery has not yet started.

## Stage One

At Stage One, recovery begins. It involves participating in a full recovery program to assist in healing the Stage Zero condition or conditions. A person may have a spiritual awakening while in Stage Zero and try to bypass this one.

## Stage Two

Stage Two is one that many people also may try to bypass. It involves healing adult child or co-dependence issues. Once a person has a stable and solid Stage One recovery—one that has lasted for at least a year or longer—it may be time to consider looking into these issues. An *adult child* is anyone who grew up in an unhealthy, troubled or dysfunctional family.[2] Many adult children may still be in a similar unhealthy environment, whether at home, in one or more relationships, or at work.

## Stage Three

Stage Three recovery is the one into which we may be compelled prematurely by having a spiritual awakening. It is the experience of spirituality and its incorporation into daily life. This is an ongoing process.

If we try to go around or bypass the darkness to get to the Light, i.e., if we try to ignore the lower to get to the higher levels of our consciousness, something—we can call it our shadow—will pull us back until we work through our particular unfinished business. Trying to avoid this work of Stages One and Two recovery can also be called *premature*

---

[2] See Appendix I for defining abuse or trauma.

*transcendence* or *high-level denial.* As Barbara Harris points out, this is seen in any number of situations, from being prematurely born again, to having a spiritual awakening and focusing only on the Light, to becoming attached to a guru or way. Its consequences are often active co-dependence: denial of the richness of our inner life; trying to control oneself or others; all-or-none thinking and behaving; feelings of fear, shame and confusion; high tolerance for inappropriate behavior; frustration, addiction, compulsion, relapse, and unnecessary pain and suffering.

The way out of this trap is to work through the pain of wherever we may be, or just enjoy the joyous feelings. Those who are actively addicted or disordered can work through a Stage One full recovery program. Those who are adult children of troubled or dysfunctional families can work through Stage Two recovery. Throughout this book Barbara is mindful of these necessities: we cannot let go of something if we do not know experientially of what we are letting go; we cannot transcend the unhealed; and we cannot connect experientially to the God of our understanding until we know our True Self, our heart.

In this book Barbara Harris breaks new ground, expanding our beliefs so we can bring our higher nature into our everyday life. Her writing is heartfelt, and she shares her own experiences comfortably, never holding herself separate from her readers. This kind of humility allows readers to experience a healing unity with her as she offers her guidance. Repeatedly she invites us to stretch beyond the limits of who we thought we were.

I recommend this book for anyone who has had a spiritual awakening of any kind, or wonders if they might have had one. Also, for anyone who would like to have one.

*Charles L. Whitfield, M.D.*
*January 1995*

# Doorways to Our Soul

This book is a guide to assist those who are opening up and experiencing, or want to experience, the mystical or heart side of their nature and the nature of the Universe. This awakening is not something to be understood logically, but through experience, perception and intuition. It is *heartfelt* experience. Our heads will have a hard time sorting through some of this, so it will help to read this with your heart as well as with your eyes and mind.

My spiritual awakening began in 1975 when I had two profound near-death experiences while critically ill and suspended in a circle bed. I was an atheist until then. So my path has led me through years of research, including six at the University of Connecticut Medical School assisting psychiatry professor Bruce Greyson with his research projects on the near-death experience (NDE). Bruce is the Director of Research for the

1

International Association for Near-Death Studies (IANDS) and a past president. He is co-editor of the book, *The Near-Death Experience: Problems, Prospects and Perspectives,* and the editor of the only scholarly journal on this subject, *The Journal of Near-Death Studies.* Bruce and I facilitated an IANDS support group together for six years. I have also worked closely with Kenneth Ring, Ph.D. He is a professor of psychology at the University of Connecticut and past president of IANDS, and is internationally known as an authority on NDEs and spiritual awakenings. I am a key subject in his now-classic book, *Heading Toward Omega: In Search of the Meaning of the Near-Death Experience.* As colleagues, Ken, Bruce and I have presented research together often over the past decade. We have theorized and written together, appeared on many TV shows and together served on the executive board of IANDS.

For the last 14 years I have given talks and workshops in the United States and Canada on the Near-Death Experience. I have also been active in the media coverage for the past ten years, including all the major TV talk, news and magazine shows, every major magazine, and the wire services. Hollywood picked up the theme in 1980 with the excellent film *Resurrection,* and more recently in *Ghost, Always, Flatliners, Defending Your Life, Almost an Angel* and others. Whether I am answering questions from an audience participant, being a consultant for a TV production or being interviewed by a reporter, always the same questions come up. Why are we here? Or, what does it all mean? My answer is the same as the thousands of experiencers of the NDE (NDErs) whom my colleagues and I have interviewed: We are here to grow psychologically and spiritually, or *psychospiritually.*

There are three ways described in this book to grow psychospiritually. I cover them here by describing them, providing some tools to conquer their obstacles and move through their changes, and offer suggestions to help in your journey.

The first way is through regular spiritual practice. Generic kinds of spiritual practice include meditation and selfless service. I will discuss spiritual practice throughout this book.

The second way is by living our life practicing unconditional love, and it overlaps the other two ways.

The third way is through a spiritual awakening, also known as Spiritual Emergence Syndrome (SES). These direct experiences of the numinous or "cosmic unity" can be triggered by a near-death experience or any one of the several others below.

## Near-Death Experiences

About one third to 40 percent of the people who come close to death report an experience beyond this reality called a near-death experience. Usually it starts with a sense of overwhelming peace, and then a lifting out of the body, or suddenly seeing the body as if above it looking down. Other stages include a place of darkness; moving through a tunnel; meeting with guides or dead relatives; seeing a Light often described as overwhelming love or God; merging with the Light; heavenly landscapes; a life review—occasionally the life review continues into the future and is called "a personal flash forward"; being given a choice to stay or go back; possibly the moment reversing, and then the return to this reality and the body.

## Childbirth

During delivery some women experience leaving their bodies and viewing the birth from high in the room. Often they report a guide or deceased relative being there and sharing their joy. Sometimes they report being transported to heavenly landscapes and being given information that they had no way of knowing. I have heard of experiences where, without leaving their bodies, they are filled with an incredible ecstasy that alleviates all pain. A sense of bliss stays with them for weeks and even longer.

Recently, when I spoke at the American Holistic Medical Association's annual convention, several physicians shared with me their experiences during childbirth. While none of these experiences were specifically NDEs, they were out-of-body and spiritual experiences. Perhaps if more women were told of this possibility, it would give them the awareness to relax into the experience and allow it to happen.

## Meditation

Many meditators report experiences after three to five years of practicing meditation. Some tell of out-of-body experiences—viewing the physical body from high in the room, usually a corner. More common is the experience of expansion, feeling oneself becoming larger, even a sense of expanding out into the Universe, but still maintaining one's identity. This happened to me occasionally. Sometimes I saw shapes resembling Hebrew or Sanskrit letters appearing as though in neon and repeated over and over to infinity. Sometimes I heard my own chuckling and the sound seemed to reverberate throughout the Universe. (See page 48 for suggestions on how to meditate.)

## Intense Prayer

Intense prayer can trigger an experience. I've heard several accounts of such experiences when emotional intensity is very high because of great fear, loss, joy or gratitude. Often repetition of a memorized prayer gives way to the feeling of communication without words, a sense of unity with a Power that understands completely without any need to go on explaining. We feel as if we have moved into a clear space beyond this reality, while physically remaining here. Then there is overwhelming peace. Whether the prayers are due to painful reasons or joy and gratitude, suddenly we sense that we have been heard and everything is all right. Even if we have never before experienced anything like this, this gentle communication is all we need to begin our spiritual awakening.

## Experiencing the Death of a Loved One

After I give a talk, at least one person, and sometimes several people, will comment that their spiritual awakening began when they were involved with the death of a loved one. I have heard amazing stories over the years, but I didn't really understand until December of 1992, when my father died with practically no warning.

He had become ill suddenly and was hospitalized in an intensive-care unit. I was told that he had leukemia, but because he had never complained and had never gone to a doctor, it took us all by surprise. In fact, my father had never missed a day of work until the afternoon before when he came home and collapsed. When I arrived at the hospital, he was in a coma. There were complications, the doctor explained, and my father would remain in a coma and probably die that day or the next.

I stood at his bedside, talking to him quietly as I stroked his forehead and hair. Within half an hour he was mumbling, then he was awake, asking questions and giving instructions for my mother's care. Occasionally he slipped into fitful sleep, then woke again to ask if he was dead yet.

When the nurses came to attend to his tubes and medications, he fought them with the same physical strength he had shown his whole life. Trays flew, and even though he was restrained, he was able to pull out his tubes and needles. He fought off pills and spat out the ones we got into his mouth, sometimes as long as 20 minutes later. Occasionally, he would tell us that his mother was there.

By 5:00 P.M. my mother, brother, my three children and I were gathered around his bed. He woke and cried quietly as he related memories of each of us, and said how much he loved us. When he was finished, he said he really wanted a corned beef sandwich. My kids ran out to the closest deli and brought back seven sandwiches. We settled down wherever we could in his room and ate together, telling stories and laughing. For those few moments, we, including my dad, forgot the weight of where we were and why. Within minutes after finishing his sandwich, my father slipped into a quiet sleep.

Soon a hospice nurse arrived and I listened as she evaluated the scene, assuring all of us that hospice could make my father more comfortable and promising my mother that, if he did get better, he could come home. We both explained to her several times that the heroic measures being used in the I.C.U. wouldn't cure him, but were painful and upsetting to him. During the ambulance ride to the hospice, Dad was in good spirits and even joked with the attendants, my brother told me later. At the hospice he swallowed the dose of morphine cooperatively. Then I massaged my father's feet. As I did, I looked into his eyes, silently telling him, telepathically I hoped, that it was all right to leave, to go to the Light, and that I loved him.

By that time it was almost midnight and we were all exhausted. I wanted to stay with him all night, but I drove my mother and brother back to my parents' apartment and fell asleep quickly on the living room sofa. At 3:30 I woke to the sound of breathing. I looked around the room. No one was there. Then the breathing stopped. At 3:35 the phone rang. My dad had just died.

## Withdrawal from Chemical Dependence

Withdrawal from chemicals can bring on a spiritual experience. Many recovering alcoholics have shared stories of their experiences with me. Bill Wilson himself, the founder of Alcoholics Anonymous, had an experience with Light while going through detox.

One of my favorite stories contains a life review and what we call a "personal flash forward." First, this man viewed his life as if watching a movie. Then the movie continued beyond the present. He had seen already how selfish his drinking had been, but now a new life was unfolding. He saw that he was going to have two beautiful children—twins, a boy and a girl. The boy looked just like him and the girl resembled the woman he knew he would meet one day and fall in love with. And that's exactly what happened. Although he didn't see his wife in his "personal flash forward," he recognized her when he met her, because she looked like his daughter.

## Bottoming Out from an Overwhelming Loss

Nancy Clark and I first met, so to speak, on the pages of Kenneth Ring's *Heading Toward Omega* as subjects. When we met in person later at IANDS board meetings, we quickly became friends. This is her story as she told it to me:

In 1979 I was delivering a eulogy for a dear friend who had been killed in an airplane crash. Shortly before the start of the service, I experienced a flow of energy beginning from my toes, moving up through my entire body and out the top of my head. Unearthly peace filled my grief-ravaged body.

As I began giving the eulogy, I became aware of a brilliant white Light radiating toward me and infiltrating my entire being with the most incomprehensible outpouring of unconditional love. I knew instinctively that I was in the presence of God and, inwardly, my soul rejoiced! I lifted out of my body and became aware that I had stepped out of the physical dimension into the real, or spiritual dimension, my true HOME.

For the duration of my experience, I was one with the Light/God and bathed in the healing power of God's perfect love. I was given a life review that focused on self understanding, not condemnation, so I could experience wholeness and behold my true spiritual nature.

I wanted to stay forever with the Light, but the Light/God communicated telepathically that no, there was work for me to do. I was to return and communicate to the world the message of love and harmony, and that there was life after death. I was given a flash forward of my life in order to see my service to God and humanity—workshops, media work, etc. Before I could agree to commit myself to this work, the Light showed me both the positive and negative aspects of the work. Again, scenes appeared. This time I saw people ridiculing me and the message I came to share. I saw those I trusted direct skepticism and sarcasm at me. It was sad to see because I knew the Light's message was one of love and healing, not harm. Again the scenes changed and the positive aspects of the work were revealed to me. I saw people listening to me, eager to explore their inner places of greater wisdom and their connectedness to the Light/God. It was heartwarming. I decided joyfully to return to this physical dimension and undertake the work for the Light/God. Once my decision was made, the Light bombarded my consciousness with total knowledge, or spiritual wisdom, so that upon my return I would be prepared to begin my service to God and humanity.

Still merged into oneness with the Light, we began to travel very fast through the vast darkness of the Universe. I was struck by the multidimensional cosmos before me, so unlike our three-dimensional world. We traveled back to the beginning of creation, where I was shown that the Light/God was the beginning of all things created and that everything had a spark of the divinity at the core of its being.

Traveling back toward the earth I was allowed to witness the world's social injustices, the wars, the sick, the oppressed. Because I was merged into oneness with the Light, I had identical consciousness as the Light, so I viewed everything through the eyes of unconditional love. I understood that everyone plays his or her part and, ultimately, everything fits into a much larger, orderly design. I saw the inter-connectedness of all things and understood on a spiritual level that we are, indeed, all one.

Just before my experience ended, the Light/God communicated additional messages to encourage me in my service to the Light and humanity. With one final hug the experience ended, and I was back in my physical body finishing the eulogy.

From that moment on, I was a changed woman. Foremost is my passionate, experiential, personal communion with God. My whole being has become intimately aware of the inward presence of God and God's love. My life of service to God and humanity always moves me in directions that accomplish this work. My personal life has been a radiant outward expression of the divine within me. Choices I make, relationships I nurture, values I hold: all serve to keep me centered in the love that sustains and the peace and joy that dwells within me.

These last three triggers to awakening spiritually—death of a loved one, withdrawal from chemical dependence and bottoming out from loss—unfortunately are through crisis and suffering. The Chinese symbol for crisis also means opportunity. Ancient Eastern spiritual literature has always recognized that liberation can be achieved during crisis and suffering. (See the section on healthy grieving, page 80.) From my audiences, I have heard about as many awakenings during a crisis as from a near-death event.

## An Alien Encounter Including Angels or Other Beings

While encounters with aliens are a controversial subject, Kenneth Ring asked me to include it in this book because, as he describes in *The Omega Project*, experiencers of alien abduction go through the same awakening journey and the same changes that I describe on these pages.

The first time I spoke up about angels was at a church in Connecticut where I was presenting a seminar on NDEs. During the coffee break, several people asked what I thought of angels and told me stories of their encounters with angels as adults. Many said that even though they were encouraged to believe in them as children, there came a time when they understood that, like Santa Claus, angels were nonsense. Yet they knew what they had seen. When the group reassembled, I reported to the audience what I had just heard. I asked how many had as adults experienced visitations from angels or other beings. With a roar of laughter, about one third of this audience raised their hands. Now I bring up the subject of guides and angels routinely at hospice talks, and receive about the same reaction.

## An Intense Transcendent Sexual Experience

In chapter 10, I will go into more depth on how to evoke this experience. For now I will give an example of a spiritual awakening where, like the others, this was not anticipated.

A typical experience might be a couple engaging in sex who have always enjoyed each other, and who are suddenly aware of a deeper sensation. First it radiates from the point of contact in the genitals and then spreading through their bodies, like ecstasy or bliss or something they cannot identify. They are able to verbalize, although briefly, because the feelings are overwhelming and move them away from speech. They feel as though they have entered a sacred temple and have become an altar to each other. They feel a kind of peace they have never experienced before. Time has no meaning. Their sense of unity with each other is complete and they also "know" God or a Higher Power is in unity with them.

Some people also report out-of-body experiences and transcending to other realities.

## Spontaneously When in Nature

Poets from the beginning of the written word have described transcendence through nature—mountain vistas, sunsets, nighttime skies, forests, lakes, walks on a shoreline. Programs like vision quests or wilderness training can create all that is necessary to have an experience. Native American celebrations that induce transcendent experiences are also offered all over the US, Mexico and Canada.

Chapter 3, "A Practical Mystic's Story," contains a spiritual awakening that happened spontaneously at Mount St. Helens.

## While Reading Spiritual Literature or Hearing a Spiritual Talk

I hear this over and over again from students of *A Course in Miracles* and members of Alcohol Anonymous when they first started in AA. Spiritual talks, especially if the speaker is charismatic, trigger awakenings, if the experiencer is ready. Stories of this kind are common when a guru from the East comes to visit. I have heard countless stories of a feeling going right through the surprised experiencer's heart, then they report falling over in bliss and spending hours in Light or feelings of ecstasy. The word given by the Eastern religions for this phenomena is *Shaktipat.* Here in the West it can be called "slain in the Holy Spirit."

## In a "Big Dream" That is Remembered for Life

My favorite story about a "big dream" happened in 1986 when *McCall's Magazine* did an article about near-death experiences, including the research and support group Bruce Greyson and I conducted. Within a month of the article being published we received 500 letters. One came from a 97-year-old woman who wrote of a dream she'd had when she was 17, that had several of the classic stages of the near-death experience. But, she wrote, it had only been a dream.

I had to telephone and hear the dream from her mouth. She retold it to me as clearly as if it had happened yesterday and she added that her entire life, all of her principles and values had come from that experience. "That dream governs the way I treat other people and myself!" she said. I asked her if she could remember other dreams that happened 80 years ago? "No," she answered. "Please," I said, "don't think of this as only a dream! Your dream and your aftereffects are just as profound as any near-death experiencers." She laughed lightly and said, "Okay" (see the Dream section in chapter 11 for ways of inducing spiritual dreams).

## A Kundalini Experience

Kundalini is a term used in the East, but full-blown experiences of Kundalini awakening are being heard more and more frequently here in the Western world. Because of this there is a group of researchers who recently have created the Kundalini Research Network to encourage and report on the scientific study of this phenomenon. Chapter 2 is from my keynote address to this group, which opened its first international conference, called "Kundalini: Dawn of a New Science." Chapter 5 has a list of signs of Kundalini opening or arousal. We have demonstrated in several research projects that experiencers have almost twice as many signs and manifestations of what we call the "Physio-Kundalini Syndrome" as do our control groups.[1]

Whether this opening or arousal happens during our original experience, or our first experience becomes a subsequent trigger for a later experience of Kundalini, is not known. And experiencers many times tell of signs and manifestations of Kundalini arousal without having a dramatic Kundalini experience at all. Anyone who desires to awaken spiritually can invite this energy into their lives to guide them through the journey of spiritual awakening. The more we read and learn, the more powerfully this energy may appear to us as signs and manifestations. At the same time, coincidence beyond the average and possibly even psychic abilities will appear (see chapter 8). Before reading on, if

---

[1] Greyson, Ring.

this is happening in your life at an overwhelming rate, turn to and read the section on the first chakra, especially the part about grounding (see pages 70-71).

A full-blown experience contains a sense of energy surging up the spine, sometimes fanning out over the upper back and shoulders. Possibly there's a roaring noise in the ears or isolated pockets of heat somewhere in the body. A sense of bliss, joy and peace fill the mind. A feeling of sweet nectar can seem to flow over the face and then energy moves through the throat, heart or navel. This is possibly described as a piercing sensation, but also pleasant. After that, or intermixed can, be incredible colors, lights, aromas and/or sounds.

## Breath and Body Work

Holotrophic breath work is a powerful way to induce and continue spiritual experiences. As with Shamanic rituals, vision quests, etc., the element of surprise or spontaneity is missing. However, many, including myself, believe that knowing you are inviting an experience leaves room for preparation and alleviates feelings afterward of worry and fear due to lack of prior knowledge or control.

I attended a workshop with Stanislav and Christina Grof, who are the creators of holotrophic breath work (you can find these workshops through the Spiritual Emergence Network listed in Appendix II). It was powerful, and I was glad to be in a protected environment all week at the Omega Institute. Dr. Grof lectured in the mornings to give us a foundation. In the afternoon, for two to three hours, half of us lay on mats and did breath work while our sitter, a chosen partner, watched over us. On alternate days breathers became sitters.

Evenings we shared our experiences of that day and the drawings we did immediately upon coming out of them. The Grofs helped us integrate what we visualized and felt. These journeys are powerful and similar to, if not the same as Shamanic journeys, rebirthing and even near-death experiences.

In one of my breathing sessions I re-experienced my birth. When the session was over, Dr. Grof and I telephoned my mother. I told her what I had experienced and she said that was exactly what had happened. Incidentally, after my birth experience I went into a "clear space." Never before had I been able to achieve clear space in meditation. Breath work showed me the way, or maybe it affirmed that it existed. I have heard about many experiences in breath work more profound than mine.

Body work is another way. All types of massage are offered today. We would need a whole book to go over the different descriptions. The type done in my practice, I developed for survivors of physical and sexual abuse. It is a slow, gentle process done at a pace that is comfortable for the client. When pain, which we see sometimes as "buried stress," is revealed in an area, the client breathes into the pain as I either massage it or send healing energy through it. The goal is to release pain and chronic stress, or energy blocks (see chapter 6). Occasionally profound experiences happen during the massage on the table or later in dreams, psychotherapy, meditation, prayer, etc.

## Gradually, Without First Having a Dramatic Experience

At meetings and talks I always hear at least once, and often several times, "I'm having all the aftereffects the rest of you are but I never had a near-death experience." What these people go on to describe is what is called "synchronicity." We have become aware of linking coincidences, evidence that our lives are woven from some higher awareness. Rationally, we know the odds are loaded against this precise coincidence happening. There is a strong recognition of higher or spiritual meaning and a sense of our being connected rather than being a single, separate and lonely person. Sometimes there is a sense of illumination, perhaps even a time shift, and we know that we truly have a place in the Universe. In looking closer to my own inner life during synchronistic moments, I realized that my ego, or false self, becomes overwhelmed and I am suddenly perceiving a much greater reality than my false self can see or wants to admit exists. (My brain's left hemisphere suspends judgment and my right hemisphere has free reign to accept and interpret a much bigger view of reality. Perhaps at these moments our True Self experiences its connection to its Higher Self and the Universe, or we become what Charles Whitfield calls the Sacred Person.)

These coincidences generate wonderful story-telling sessions that can continue from one person to the next, relating how they happened to be guided to this particular talk—sometimes after "just happening" to be given or finding my book *Full Circle*, or Kenneth Ring's *Heading Toward Omega*. I have heard instances of a book literally falling off the shelf and hitting them.

At support group meetings, many times we have agreed that synchronicity is a much gentler way to awaken spiritually than some of the more disconcerting possibilities. The near-death experience, especially for an atheist as I was, has been compared to being "hit over the head with a two-by-four!" Most agree that it would be easier to read a book like this one and make a conscious choice to awaken spiritually.

Inviting synchronicity into your life is a way to grow and awaken that gradually and gently does the same work as the experiences I have just described. As you read through these pages, if you haven't started your journey yet, just ask. Prayer is a way of starting. Be specific. Visualize it happening. I share a story in chapter 9 about the power of prayer and how I became introduced to this energy that can be called many things—Kundalini, Divine Energy, Holy Spirit, Ruach Ha

Kodesh (the Holy Wind)—that guides my life and is my life. When it is invited into your life, it will show you too how to see from a higher point of view.

## Our Dove Story

People have told me their stories of spiritual awakening while reading spiritual books, about "getting zapped" by a certain passage. I've studied *A Course in Miracles* for a few years and I've wished a passage would open up like that for me, but it remained a beautiful collection of poetic and informative thoughts about the Holy Spirit until recently.

Every morning after breakfast, Charlie and I sit on our sun porch and read a lesson from *A Course in Miracles*. Each time we walk out onto the porch we must walk beneath a beautiful stained glass window that we rescued from a remodeling sale in an old church. The stained glass portrays a white dove, symbol of the Holy Spirit.

One day something startling happened. In the morning we had read a lesson that hadn't made much sense to me, so when I came home from the office that evening, I went out on the porch to read it again. The meaning of the words jumped out at me. I felt super-charged, filled with joy. My near-death experience had given me an understanding that I'd never been able to articulate before, and now, here it was, in a book in my hands. When Charlie came home I read the lesson to him joyfully and explained its relationship to my understanding of my near-death experience: *We can think as God thinks by creating our shift in perception through forgiveness*. In that forgiveness, our False Self or negative ego is diminished and our True Self, who we are *authentically*, is energized.[2]

---

[2] I will get back to the subject of forgiveness again, but for now I want to say something about forgiveness and timing. Forgiveness is a soul process, a process of the heart, the True Self, that takes time and results in a feeling of release or lifting away of heaviness. If we forgive too soon because it's something we *should* do or the *right* thing to do, it remains a head trip, an intellectual exercise that feels forced, and it's not authentic (see page 45).

The next morning I wandered out onto the porch again, thinking that I would pick up the book and read that particular lesson again. As I reached out my hand for the book, I was thinking that this book contains the Holy Spirit. As my hand touched the book, I was startled by a loud thud on the glass door. I looked up, and saw a dove had smacked into the window and then I saw it shake out its feathers and fly off. Charlie came in response to my call and together we noticed the beautiful imprint of the dove's wings and body left on the glass. He took several pictures of the dove's imprint. The photos show the dove in a glowing white outline.

## Warning: This Book Is Not Logical

It's amazing after an awakening to realize suddenly that we are spiritual beings learning to have a human experience.[3] Our brains reel with new information. Chapter 7 gives a simplified explanation of our brain-shift to help us feel comfortable with this kind of knowledge, information and wisdom that doesn't flow in a linear or logical fashion.

Spiritual awakenings have been written about throughout recorded history. They are described in *The Tibetan Book of the Dead*, *The Egyptian Book of the Dead*, the Bible, Native American folklore and others. Previously, religion served as a *bridge* to the spiritual. In modern times, mainstream Western religions have rejected spiritual experiences as a reality. Direct sensing of spirit in our lives is compatible with religion, however, if *we* choose to make it so. Unfortunately, over the centuries we were taught to worship the bridge—religion—and sever ourselves from spirit, thus severing ourselves from a big part of who we are. Traditional psychiatry also has often confused spiritual experiences with psychosis and tried to use suppressive drugs to control them. Both science and religion

---

[3] Small, 1991

have created a schism in Western culture. This schism between our physical and spiritual aspects has kept us locked developmentally into a slot called "normal." However, once we experience, or even want to experience our spiritual nature, "normal" becomes obsolete and wholeness becomes our goal.

This book does not promise enlightenment. That is a process between you, your Higher Self and God. But it may help you through some of life's big and little bumps as you begin to discover a life of peace and joy that is shared with the ones you love and those you may choose to help. I have been living this book for almost two decades now, and hundreds of you have added to my gathering of this information by your sharing.

As a spiritual teacher, I have been fortunate these past years to teach at universities, hospices, hospitals and for a variety of organizations, including Rutgers University's School of Alcohol and Drug Studies, The Jung Institute, The International Transpersonal Association, The Institute of Transpersonal Psychology, The Kundalini Research Network and A Course In Miracles Community Network.

Much of my knowledge has also come from facilitating other IANDS support groups. I was able to sort out much of my own personal "stuff" from what is universal to all of us. The personal stories I am about to tell are a reflection of the numbers of us who shared, not just about me or some of my friends. Because I am a clinician as well as a researcher and experiencer, each chapter's voice will change accordingly. Some chapters are chatty, with a story format, while other chapters are technical sounding and harder to digest. I am confident that the changing format won't be a problem for most readers because of the hundreds of you I have met who have reported your increased ability to understand and assimilate information and knowledge as soon as you asked for it, plus an insatiable appetite to learn.

The most important step to ease our journey is described on these pages and between the lines.[4] This threesome of our True Self, Higher Self and God, which Charles Whitfield calls the "Sacred Person," has our blueprint. Just as the acorn contains the giant oak tree, we too contain the plan to develop to our full potential. We, you and I, must ask the energy called Divine, Holy, Higher Self or Kundalini, and God or the Universe to work with us, to co-create together, to bring us to wholeness and help us experience living every day in the now with God's love.

My hope in writing this book is to help you enjoy the blessings, work through the obstacles and commit to your spiritual journey in your own way. Forgive me for not dissecting and analyzing in logical order what to our logical side always has been and probably always will be a Divine Mystery. The only way to understand all this is to live it. Refer back to this book when you feel confused, overwhelmed or stuck. Eventually you may notice that the journey has smoothed out and you're living life as a Practical Mystic in and with unconditional love.

---

[4] This most important step is when we communicate to ourselves and the Universe our eagerness to commit to our spiritual journey. The journey begins in our spiritual awakening, or *it can begin at this moment through our willingness.*

## Timeless Zone

I'm walking around in this reality
Somewhat confused!
I have resided in more than one
And physical reality puzzles me more
Than the "altered states" I have played in.

Confusions arise here
As beliefs drop away.
All the dichotomies come crashing down
And opposites dance on the same continuum.

Sometimes, not to be recommended—
While going through pain.
But probably the quickest way to go.

To Exist is not to live—
But just "to exist."
To live, really LIVE—
You have to dive in
And swim around in IT!

When the Doors of perception—
Finally clear,
The awareness of living in the NOW.
Timeless NOW.

So this is what they call "Cosmic Consciousness."
First it comes in flashes—
Then interludes.
Finally, an understanding of
GRACE.

And what GOD is—
Where I wind up at the end of all my words.

*BHW*

# Spiritual Awakenings– My Personal Story

*T his chapter is edited from a keynote address given June 17, 1992 for the first annual Conference of the Kundalini Research Network (KRN) entitled "Kundalini: Dawn of a New Science." This pioneering conference was attended by over 100 physicians and scientists. This was an international group, many of whom have authored papers and books on Spiritual Emergency, Spiritual Emergence Syndrome and Kundalini Awakening. As they gave their papers, many also shared their personal experiences. See Appendix II for more information on KRN.*

About 20 years ago I irritated an existing curvature in my spine. What followed was two years of conservative care for back pain—which meant a lot of Valium. I started by taking five milligrams, and then increased to ten mg four times a day. I was also given Empirin with codeine and eventually Percodan. I was hospitalized four times for traction and Demerol, as required. On the third and fourth hospitalization a procedure called a rhizotomy—interruption of the roots of the spinal nerves within the spinal canal—was performed to kill sensory nerves in my lumbar spine. But the back pain continued.

By the fourth hospitalization they put me in a full body cast—from under my arms to my knees—which I lived in for a month. If the body cast stopped the pain, then I was to go back in for a spinal fusion. If immobilizing my spine with a cast stopped the pain, they reasoned, then immobilizing my spine from within—fusing the vertebrae—would stop the pain permanently. My x-rays had shown congenital scoliosis (spinal curvature) with spondylolisthesis (forward displace-ment of one vertebra over another). What my x-rays didn't show was a fracture in one of my vertebrae. That was finally diagnosed during a surgery that was scheduled for two hours and took five and a half.

When I woke the next day I was in a Stryker frame circle bed, which is a pretty awesome way to wake up from surgery. There were two big chrome hoops and a stretcher suspended in the middle, with me in it. It looks like a ferris wheel for one. Three times a day nurses would put pillows and anoth-er stretcher over me, strap me down and then rotate me onto my face. There I stayed for 20 minutes to a half hour, so my lungs could drain and the skin on my back could air-dry. They would put pillows over me before they rotated me onto my stomach because I was so thin I couldn't tolerate the hardness of the stretcher. Normally, I weighed 118. Then I weighed 83 pounds, so you can just imagine how skinny I was. It had been a long, hard two years.

## My Spiritual Awakenings

About two days after surgery, complications set in and I started to die. I remember waking up in the circle bed and seeing this huge belly. I had swelled up, and I remember thinking, I must be having another baby. As I considered it further, I realized the swelling was pulling, and it hurt. I had two huge incisions in my back and the swelling was pulling those incisions open. That pain wasn't like any labor pain I'd ever had. First I started calling out, then I was screaming.

People came rushing in. It was a dramatic scene like you see on TV. Everybody running in, pushing carts and machinery, throwing things back and forth over me. They hooked me up to all kinds of machinery, tubes and bags. I didn't become a respiratory therapist until several years later, so I had no idea what was going on, but I knew I wanted to die.

After two years on Valium, which relaxed my muscles but draped me in a veil of deep depression, I was bitter. I didn't want to go on living as I had been. I had three young children at home and I certainly wasn't functioning as their mother anymore. Also, after going through a lot of abuse as a child, I had given up on God when I was about eight or nine. I was an atheist. The night before surgery a priest had come in to visit me. I remember telling him that if there really was a God, he could tell his God to fix my back. But if his God couldn't do that, I really wanted to die. The priest looked at me sadly and walked out as I thought about my black-and-white decision—restoration or death.

So I screamed at the hoard of hurrying people with their monitors, bottles, pumps and equipment, "No! No! No! Leave me alone. Let me die!" Then I blacked out.

## First Near-Death Experience

I awoke out in the hall in the middle of the night. I looked up and down the hall and didn't see anybody. The lights were dim. It was quiet. I remember thinking that I'd be in trouble if they caught me out in the hall, because I was suppose to be suspended in the bed. So I turned around to go back into my room and found myself looking directly at a public-address speaker. That wasn't possible, I thought. It was at least three feet above my head. I moved into my room and looked down at the circle bed and saw me. I chuckled. It struck me as funny because "she" looked funny with white tape around my nose holding in a tube. I was out of pain. I felt calm in a way I had never felt before, so I hung out with "her" awhile.

Next, I was in total blackness. I didn't know how I got there. Then I felt hands come around me and pull me into lush warmth. I realized it was my grandmother. She was pulling me into her. She had been dead for 14 years and I never had before considered her existing beyond her death. I never even thought of considering it. But I knew I was with her, and I realized that everything that I had believed in the past was not, or might not, be real. Maybe my belief systems were really messed up, but this was real and everything else had been an illusion.

And as I thought that, there was a sudden replay of every scene my grandmother and I had shared during our 19 years together. It wasn't just my memories of her; it was also her memories of me, and our memories became one. I could feel and see and sense exactly what she was feeling, seeing and sensing. And I'm sure she was getting the same thing from my memories. It was both of us together replaying everything that we meant to each other. It was wonderful.

I stayed with her for a while. Then I started moving away. At that time I wouldn't have called where I was a tunnel, but later I realized that "tunnel" is the closest word. Whatever it was that I was moving through started off totally black. Then I became aware that there was an energy churning through the blackness. As I watched the energy move, shades of gray to almost white separated from the churning—out of the darkness was coming Light, and the Light was moving way ahead of me—far, far ahead.

My hands were expanding. They felt like they were becoming infinitely large. A breeze was wrapped around my body and I could hear a low droning noise that beckoned me. And I was moving along.

Then I was back in my body, it was morning and I was back in the circle bed. Two nurses came into my room to open the drapes. The light blinded me and I asked them to close the drapes again. My eyes had become super-sensitive to light; the drapes stayed closed the entire month I was there. Also, I had them keep the door closed because my hearing had become super-sensitive.

I told the two morning staff nurses that I had left the bed in the middle of the night—I didn't tell them what I just told you because, in the beginning, I had no words for any of this.

"I left the bed," I told them.

"No, no, you didn't leave the bed," one of them said.

"You don't understand. I left the bed. I was out in the hall."

"No, no, you hallucinated," they insisted.

About the fourth time we went around about this, they sedated me.

As my physicians came and went through the day, I told them. All of them said I had hallucinated, except my internist. He sat down and listened. Then he wrote his home phone number on my tissue box and said, "I don't know what happened to you. I've never heard of this before. But if it happens again, call me."

## Life Review

About a week later it happened again. I wasn't critically ill anymore. They rotated me forward onto my face. I was very uncomfortable. I seemed to be in that position forever. The nurse didn't return to rotate me back, so I reached for the call button, but it had slipped away from the sheet. I started to call, then yell, then scream frantically, but my door was closed. No one came. I began to wet the bed. Then I separated from my body, just as I had when I was being abused as a child—but I hadn't remembered until that moment.[1]

As I left my body, I went out into the darkness. Looking down and off to the right, I saw myself in a bubble—in the circle bed crying. Then I looked up and to the left and I saw my year-old self in another bubble, face-down in my crib, crying just as hysterically. I looked to the right, to the left, back and forth about three times, then I let go. I decided I didn't want to be her anymore; I'd go to the baby. As I did, I became aware that energy was wrapping around me and going through me, permeating me, holding up every molecule of my being.

It was not an old man with a long white beard. It took me a long time to use the word God. In fact, I never used any word until I saw the movie *Star Wars* and they talked about The Force. I was already reading quantum physics, trying to figure out how I could explain what permeated me and was me . . . and all of us. It was there and it was holding me. I realize now that without It, I wouldn't have had the strength to experience what I am about to explain to you.

I, we, went to the baby. Picture that baby in the center bubble in a cloud of bubbles that contained thousands and thousands of bubbles. In each bubble was another event from my life. As we went to the baby, it was as if we were bobbing through the bubbles. At the same time there was a linear sequence in which I relived 32 years of my life. I could hear myself saying, "No wonder, no wonder. No wonder you are the way you are now. Look what was done to you when you were a little girl."

I saw all the abuse. But I didn't see it in little bits and pieces the way I had remembered it as an adult. Not only was I me; I was my mother. And my dad. And my brother. We were all one. I realized that we don't end at our skin. We are

---

[1] Kenneth Ring discusses dissociation in his paper, "The Omega Project" and in his third book of the same name. See pages 38-39 for a summation.

all this big churning mass of consciousness. We are all one. And my mother physically abusing me came from the abuse that she had received as a child. Her rage came from her childhood and might have been given to me, but not on purpose. My father was too confused and numb to stop it. When my brother raged at me, it was because he was getting rage from my mother. I was realizing that I wasn't the only victim; we were all victims.

And as I kept hearing myself say "No wonder," I was growing up and getting married and having my children and seeing that I was on the edge of repeating the cycle. So it was "No wonder, no wonder." And at the same time, I had an amazing realization that this energy holding me had intelligence that was phenomenal. This energy was never judging me through all of it because It is not capable of judging. I was doing the judging, we judge ourselves. I realized that the only big mistake I had made in my life of 32 years was that I had never learned to love myself, but I had still judged myself as bad when I wasn't.

And then I was back, but not in my body. I was behind the nurses' station. I saw a metal circle with pillows tossing behind glass. They were the pillows I had urinated on. I was watching them in a dryer. I heard two nurses talking about me and how my day nurse was so upset after she found me, they had sent her home early. Then they were saying that I was going to be in a body cast for six months, even though they had told me six weeks, because my doctors felt that I couldn't handle the idea of being in it for six months. So they were not going to tell me the truth.

Then I was back in my body. The same two nurses I had just heard came in to check on me and I said to them, "I left the bed again."

"No, honey. You're hallucinating."

I was on no drugs at this point and I insisted, "No, I'm not hallucinating. I left the bed."

"No, you're hallucinating. You can't leave the bed."

"Please call my day nurse and tell her I'm okay," I responded. "I'm not angry with her. I know she was sent home early. And don't lie to me by telling me I'm going to be in a body cast for six weeks. Tell me the truth. I know I'm going to be in a body cast for six months. And you should have washed those pillows before you put them in the dryer. I don't care for myself, but I care for the next patient."

Then they sedated me. I learned not to talk about leaving the bed.

## Trying to Make Sense of It All

A few weeks later I came home. My cast weighed 30 pounds, I weighed 82. I needed answers to what happened. I wanted to know what had happened to me when I left the bed. What I really wanted was to be honest. I wanted to reach out to my parents and tell them everything was okay. I wanted to tell them that I loved them. I wanted to let everybody know I was all right, but for some strange reason I couldn't communicate with anybody.

After two or three months in the body cast, I asked to see a psychiatrist. My family was horrified. There was just no way that anybody was going to let me see a psychiatrist because that was something to be ashamed of. My mother had been in and out of psychiatric hospitals when I was a child, so this was a hard thing for them to face. My husband wouldn't take me. Finally, I convinced my brother. He came over one day and loaded me into his station wagon, sliding me into the back like I was a piece of furniture. I was using a walker at that point, and when we got to the psychiatrist's office, I waddled in. I could barely walk.

The psychiatrist had my medical records and he held them up—this was before microfilm—and they had to be a foot thick. "Barbara, if I had been through what you've been through, I would need to see a psychiatrist, too."

"Thank God," I thought. "He is going to understand." It took me six sessions to have the courage finally to tell him what I just told you.

He listened patiently. "You know, you have been through a lot and your job now is to go home and heal. Your job now is to go home and take your medication and when you are out of the body cast and when you are through with physical therapy, come back." He was a psychoanalyst. He told me we would go back later into my childhood. He told me that right now I had to rest and heal, and he gave me antidepressants.

More pills. At home, I waddled into the bathroom and saw 15 or so bottles. I had three different kinds of tranquilizers and sleeping pills, an assortment of pain pills, and now I had anti-depressants. But I was not depressed. I was overwhelmed, obviously overwhelmed. I was also confused. I was not depressed. How could I be depressed when I knew there was a God?

I looked in the mirror. That should have made me depressed. I was white as a sheet, I weighed so little, and suddenly I realized how bad I looked. I took out some rouge and started putting it on my face, and then I recognized my mother's image in the mirror. I was turning out just like her. My mother was always addicted to prescription drugs and worked at least five physicians and four or five pharmacies at a time. Here I was with 15 bottles of pills and a body cast and looking just like her. I started opening pill bottles and poured them into the toilet. I flushed 15 or so bottles of pills away.

The body cast came off at five and a half months. That was the beginning of the rest of my life. Although I couldn't tell anybody what had happened, I felt invincible. Then I started having headaches.[2] Besides the headaches, I found myself in weird positions. I had never heard of yoga, but I moved naturally into these strange positions. Also, while lying on the

---

[2] We know now that migraine headaches are experienced sometimes after an awakening, especially if there's an arousal of Kundalini energy.

couch reading, I felt like my whole body lifted off the couch. It felt as though energy pushed through me and lifted me up. I felt isolated pockets of heat in different parts of my body. I felt bliss rushing through me. I thought it was because I had been in a body cast. I saw a flashing light in the middle of the night. I woke my husband and ask him if he saw lightning. He'd look out and tell me the moon and stars were shining. My internist started a workup for migraines.

Around the same time, I volunteered at the hospital where I'd had my surgery. I knew that I couldn't connect with my family. I felt different and I knew it. I gave up Junior League and other community work except Brownies and Cub Scouts.

My first day volunteering at the hospital was in the emergency room. Naturally I woke up with a splitting headache. I attributed it to the excitement and went to the hospital anyway. When I got to the emergency room, I was so happy to be there. One of the first patients wheeled in was an old woman who obviously was in the process of dying—at least it was obvious to me. One of the ER physicians asked me to go to the warmer and get a blanket to cover her up because she was shivering. I put the first one on her and smoothed it out, then a second one. As I started to smooth it, something wonderful happened: the headache drained into my shoulders, down my arms and out of my hands. As I watched, her color got better and her shivering stopped. Then she told me that her pain had subsided. I sat and held her hand for the longest time.

That was the beginning of my work with dying patients. Nothing could keep me away. One day a week of volunteering turned into two and then three. They knew if they needed me a fourth day, they could call and I would come. That was when I realized that I needed to go back to school and become a nurse. But instead of a nurse, I became a respiratory therapist because I liked what they did. They are all over the hospital for codes. When someone's heart stops, they are paged to where the action is.

Unfortunately, my ideas of helping people die and the hospital's ideas were different. This was in the late 1970s and I was living and working in South Florida. I tried a Jewish hospital for a while, because I am Jewish, but that didn't work out. So I went to work in a Catholic hospital, figuring they would know. They didn't know either.

I started doing home care for the dying. I had wonderful experiences working with dying people. I still couldn't connect with my family. They thought I was really weird. But I could connect with my dying patients. They would tell me about their experiences as they lay dying. Sometimes three, four, even six months before death, they had experiences of Light.

To help them relax I meditated with them. I put my right hand on their belly and my left hand over their heart or forehead, and we meditated together for 15 or 20 minutes. Sometimes they saw and shared scenes from childhood, like stories of Brooklyn at the turn of the century. Sometimes we did life reviews together. It was a wonderful time for me.

## Heading Toward Omega

Then I read about Kenneth Ring, a professor from the University of Connecticut, in *Omni* magazine. He talked about "core" experiences, people who came close to death or died and were brought back to life and experienced reaching their core. He listed stages of this experience, including a wonderful sense of peace, out-of-body experience, going through a tunnel, seeing a Light, becoming one with the Light, meeting with dead relatives and even a life review before returning to this realm. I knew my patients were also having this experience. I wrote to him right away and said I agreed with everything he said in *Omni* but I wanted him to know that it wasn't rare. I told him it is happening everywhere all the time because of modern medical technology bringing people back. Ken wrote me and asked me to tell him more.

I wrote to him that in my own life review I remembered that I used to go to the tunnel when I was a child. Every time I was physically abused, I cried and I would wind up in the tunnel. But I didn't remember, until I was in the tunnel again and had the life review. We exchanged more letters. Coincidentally, he came to South Florida three months later and we got together at a conference, but we didn't have much time to talk. We continued our correspondence, and Ken came back three months after that for a fund-raiser in Palm Beach, seeking funding for his research. He had about an hour to spend with me and then he was going to go to a dinner meeting. I met him in the lobby of the Palm Beach Holiday Inn, took one look at him and realized he was exhausted.

"Ken, you look tired. Do you want to skip the hour and just go to your room and rest?"

"No, I want to talk with you."

That's typical of Ken, I learned. He's always there for experiencers. I told him that if he was going to take his one free hour and give it to me, I wanted him to know that I had massage oil in my purse. (I always carry oil for my patients or whoever needs a massage. Even when I worked in a hospital, during my lunch hour or after my shift I would go and massage my patients.) "You look tired, so let me give you a massage, okay?"

We went up to Ken's room and about ten minutes after I got my hands on his shoulders and neck he asked, "Have you ever heard the word Kundalini? You've got this energy coming from your hands that's called Kundalini energy. I can feel it radiating from your hands. Do me a favor and find some books on Kundalini and let me know what you think."

I had gone to a conference in Washington, D.C., two months earlier because I wanted to hear Elizabeth Kübler-Ross speak. The conference was called *Healing in Our Times.* It was put on by Sufis. I knew about none of this and even if I'd heard the word Kundalini, I would have ignored it. If I'd been told that I was a healer, I would have denied it. I came from a straight background and considered myself scientific, but this kept happening to me. I couldn't deny my experiences, but neither was I talking about them.

At the *Healing in Our Times* conference I wandered into a meditation workshop on Kundalini, but I didn't know the word. For two hours I did breath work, where we were breathing in love and breathing it out, breathing in love and breathing it out. We expanded it from the room to the hotel to the city to the country to the whole Earth, and this felt really good. When I opened my eyes there were about 30 of us still sitting there, kind of motionless. The other 200 people had left. Somebody was playing a classical piece on a grand piano in front. I remember wandering out behind the Shorham Hotel and the whole world looking like a fairyland. I remember wandering back up to my room and just falling into bed and opening my eyes in the middle of the night and watching balls of colors shooting through the room and just enjoying it. I was so peaceful and relaxed. I finally realized that my breath was down to maybe two or three inhalations a minute, and then there was a voice telling me to start breathing again. I barely had a pulse, so I brought myself out of it.

A few days after the workshop I bought a few books and as I read, I realized that the breath work in D.C. was about Kundalini. I looked at my workshop notes from the Sufi conference and there was Kundalini mentioned in different ways. Ken Ring's question had stimulated me to put the information together.

The first book I read was *Kundalini, Evolution and Enlightenment*, edited by John White. In it I read a paper by Itzak Bentov. I got his book, *Stalking the Wild Pendulum*. Everything came together. All of the signs of Kundalini, all of the symptoms—he described the whole thing. I wrote to Ken

and he wrote back. Then I called him at the University of
Connecticut and said that I thought it was time I went up
there. I had things to tell him.

"Barbara," he said, "a letter went out to you two days ago
inviting you up here. I would like to interview you for my
next book." We agreed that I would come in October.

I started having a lot of arguments with myself. The left
hemisphere of my brain would say, "Who do you think you
are, going up to tell a college professor what you know?" The
right hemisphere would respond, "I know what I know. And
I have to tell him."

Around this time I started meditating purposefully. I had
been meditating naturally since my NDE but didn't know that
was what it was called. Now I was setting aside a certain time
every day to meditate and try several different forms. I
remember getting a tape called "Angelic Music" by Iasos, a
Greek composer, and I meditated with the side entitled "The
Angels of Comfort." In the middle of the tape I popped out
of my body and looked down at myself, just the way I did in
my near-death experience. It is wonderful music and sounds
like what I heard in the tunnel.[3]

As I watched myself sitting in a semi-lotus position, I realized how quiet the house was. The stereo was off, the filter
from the swimming pool was off, the air conditioning was off
and so were all the ceiling fans and lights. I popped back into
my body and after a few minutes of looking around, I realized
that the main circuit breaker in the house had shut down.
Later when I listened to the tape, I heard a loud clicking all
the way through it. When I brought the tape to Ken, he said
that's what happens when people like me get near electrical
equipment, especially when we meditate. We activate circuit
breakers, stop computers and blow street lights. In his writings he called us "Electrical Sensitives."

---

[3] In a study, this music was chosen by hundreds of experiencers as the
music that sounds most like the music they heard or felt during their NDE.

The day before I was to fly up to Connecticut, I was still debating whether I should go. I went out into our back yard, faced the lake, spread my blanket and meditated. For the first time in meditation, I saw a face. I didn't recognize it, but it was talking to me. I wasn't pleased about that, because I didn't want to become a medium. That kind of stuff scared me.

After 20 minutes I went back into the house, trying to figure out whose face I had seen. As I pondered, I picked up a book I had just bought to read on the plane. It was Itzak Bentov's second book, *A Cosmic Book: On the Mechanics of Creation*, which his wife, Mirtala, had published after he died. I remembered feeling so disappointed when I heard he had died, because I had wanted to meet him. As I laid the book face down in my bag, I saw Bentov's picture on the back cover and was overwhelmed to recognize him as the man I had just seen in meditation. Since that day, I've seen him a few times in lucid dreams.

That was too much for my traditional background. As I flew up to Connecticut I told myself that I would tell Ken Ring immediately about seeing Bentov. If he told me I was nuts, I was going to get right back on the plane and go home. Ken met me as I got off the plane. I had the book in my hands and I said nervously, "Ken, I have to tell you . . . I saw Bentov yesterday when I was meditating."

Ken just smiled at me. He knew how much I loved Bentov's work. "Oh, Barbara, he's been seen all over Boston. It's okay." Then I knew it was all right. The left hemisphere of my brain quieted down.

I stayed in Ken's home, which he calls the Near-Death Hotel because so many near-death experiencers have come there to visit and be interviewed. Actually, it was a quaint, 200-year-old New England house overlooking a stream. We talked for the next four days. On the fourth day of interviewing, Ken turned on the tape recorder while I answered his questions for four and a half hours. That recorded material became 12½ typed pages of quotes that he used in *Heading Toward Omega*. I told him everything that I had experienced, and everything I thought I knew, and everything that sounded familiar from what I read.

At the end of the four days, Ken took me to the airport, thanked me, and then asked me to start IANDS support groups in Florida.[4] Within a few months I had two IANDS support groups started. I was glad Ken had said something, because once the groups were started, I found I really needed them, too. In fact, there never has been a support group that I have facilitated that I personally didn't need also.

At the same time, my marriage was falling apart. We had a traditional 22-year marriage, and it was obvious that there was just no way that this stuff was going to be part of that relationship. My husband was afraid of death and didn't want to talk about my experience, death or any combination of the two. For me to stay married, I would have had to go back to the way I was before my near-death experience. To do that would have meant surrendering the authentic self I was becoming. We were at an impasse.

The galleys of *Heading Toward Omega* came out the same week my marriage ended. At the same time, my parents moved in with me until they found an apartment in South Florida, and I went up to Connecticut for an IANDS board meeting. Ken's book told clearly about my memories of childhood abuse. That terrified me. Other than the book *Mommy Dearest*, nobody had talked about child abuse. I was ashamed of my disclosure. My parents were living with me, temporarily, Ken Ring's book would be released soon and I didn't know what I was going to do. I prayed a lot, and then I found out a little later that my parents weren't interested in reading Ken's book, so I was beating myself up for nothing; but it was a nerve-wracking time.

---

[4] Again, IANDS is the International Association for Near Death Studies.

When *Heading Toward Omega* came out, I was invited to speak at a church in Chevy Chase, Maryland. I talked about my NDE for 45 minutes, and afterward about a dozen people came up to talk with me. They all had been abused as children and had some kind of spiritual experience. Maybe not close to death, but their experiences were similar to mine, including the peace and sense of unity with something greater than themselves, and occasionally an out-of-body experience. Everywhere I went, people came up and told me that they also had been abused as kids, told me about their spiritual experiences, and thanked me for speaking up in *Heading Toward Omega*. Many of those people were hospice workers. It seems that a lot of us gravitate to death and dying or to some kind of health care or selfless service.

It's important to point out here that not everyone I've met who has had a spiritual experience tells me that they were abused or traumatized as a child. However, well over half of them have told me of abuse, and all of them have told me of aftereffects from awakening spiritually that changed them emotionally, psychologically, spiritually and sometimes physically.

So what began as a curse and a family secret became the greatest gift for me, because of the affirmation and support I received from others. We didn't feel the animosity anymore and we didn't feel victimized, either. What we felt, or wanted to feel, was a connection to God and the need for direction for our strong sense of mission. Where do we go from here? We all talked about an incredible sense of overwhelming love that we wanted to give to others. What do we do with it? We talked about migraine headaches and lights flashing in the night and hot hands. Let me see anybody who looks like they don't feel well and my hands heat up. We talked about energy rushing through our bodies, especially our spines or our hands, and we looked at our hands in amazement while we talked. We had inklings and gifts of healing, yet we didn't know all the details, including how to finish the process of healing ourselves.

At that point, Bruce Greyson was offered a position at the University of Connecticut, and he needed a research assistant. I was lucky enough to move up to Connecticut and assist him in the research for several years on near-death experiences. The first year we had a grant to study "suicide ideation and the near-death experience." But I was saying "Kundalini— let's look at it!" and we did.

The child abuse/trauma question kept coming up, and we avoided it. We pushed it to the background because NDEs are so great to work with by comparison. It's fun to "hang out with God." It's a great place to be. But to study child abuse or neglect or incest is painful.

I remember really impressing all this on Ken Ring one night at dinner. "We need to look at the childhood abuse factor," I said. "There is something going on here." So he put the childhood abuse/trauma factor (the loss of a sibling or parent, illness, war, etc.) in his next research project, "The Omega Project Questionnaire," and the results were revealing.[5] There was a much higher rate of incidence of childhood abuse and/or trauma among near-death experiencers than the control group.

This new child abuse/trauma factor moved Ken Ring to theorize about dissociation—obviously, I went into the tunnel; I know where I went.[6] If somebody in the field of psychology or psychiatry wants to call it dissociation, yes, it was dissociation; but it was much more. It is a special place or

---

[5] Ring and Rosing conducted a mail questionnaire survey with 74 near-death experiencers (NDErs) and 54 persons who were interested in near-death experiences but had never had one (control group). The purpose of this survey was to assess the role of psychological and developmental factors in influencing susceptibility to NDEs or alternate realities, and to measure after-effects stemming from the experience.

[6] We know now that strong emotional pain can trigger an out-of-body experience and possibly more stages. Many "old paradigm" clinicians would interpret my description as dissociation. Ring and Rosing discussed this in great

dimension beyond this reality where I could go that is real and familiar. From dissociating I learned the skill of absorption. In order to have the ability to move from one reality to the next, we must know from experience how to be absorbed, to ignore distraction and focus on alternate or subtle realities.[7] So the curse in childhood of being abused or traumatized becomes the gift in adulthood of the ability to become absorbed in alternative realities. This is one of Ring's theories in his book *The Omega Project,* and in his paper of the same name in the *Journal of Near-Death Studies.*

## Full Circle

About the same time, my first book, *Full Circle,* was released and I was on "Larry King Live." During the broadcast a physician in Baltimore, Maryland, named Charles Whitfield was watching. He remembered me from a conference about six years prior. He was coming up to Connecticut the next weekend to speak at a conference, so he called and invited me to come to the conference and to have dinner with him. Before I met with him, I thought I should at least open his book that he mailed me two or three years earlier. (I am on the editorial board of the *Journal of Near-Death Studies,* and many authors mail books to me because they want them reviewed. I look at a few, but not all of them.)

---

detail in their paper. In summarizing they said, "[What is] the core defining feature of the NDE-prone personality? In our judgement, it is the capacity to shift into states of consciousness that afford access to alternative or non-ordinary realities coupled with strong tendencies toward psychological absorption. That is, the person who is especially likely to register and recall an NDE is one whose awareness is easily able to transcend the sensory world and enter into focused attention to interior states. Once the shift to non-sensory realities has occurred, it seems to be the capacity for psychological absorption that is crucial."

[7] Meditation is a safe and easy way to develop absorption skills. Some people are born with this talent and/or their parents nurtured their creativity in childhood.

When I read Whitfield's book, *Healing the Child Within*, a whole new world opened up for me, because it was about being an adult child from a dysfunctional family.

There was a significant and easily understood chapter on post-traumatic stress disorder (PTSD). I knew so many of us had a mild to moderate PTSD from childhood experiences and/or from the event that triggered our spiritual awakening; but rather than doing the healing work necessary, a lot of us were doing what we now call "spiritual bypass." That is, we were bypassing our psychological and emotional wounds, failing to do the work to heal them, trying to live in a less painful spiritual realm where we could "hang out with God."

In *Healing the Child Within*, Whitfield showed those of us who were doing near-death studies that we didn't have to reinvent the wheel of how to heal our core, which he calls our *Child Within*. In order to feel connected to God or the Universe here, in this reality, it's important not to ignore, but to heal our wounds. As he explains in the foreword of this book, Stage Two, or adult child healing, is the way to heal our relationship to our Higher Self and God. These become one relationship, which he calls the "Sacred Person." If we don't do our healing or inner work, our connection to our Higher Self and God is intellectual and cognitive: a head trip that lacks the spiritual dimension. When we heal our True Self, our Child Within, then we experience our connection to God as we did in our spiritual experiences.[8] This is a heartfelt experience that we live every day with, and in, the here and now.

## The Twelfth Step

I have met many people since who had a spiritual experience first and then started working a Twelve Step program

---

[8] This is what Ken Ring calls our core, the part of us that has a core experience. See The Child Within in Appendix I.

because they thought they were addicted to something or knew they were adult children of dysfunctional families. At Rutgers University's School of Alcohol and Drug Studies, I teach a course on spiritual awakenings called "When The Twelfth Step Happens First." My students, who are psychotherapists and counselors, say that spiritual experiences and their aftereffects are coming up in their practices with their patients and clients, and also in their own personal lives.[9]

What we are reporting on at this first Kundalini Research Network conference—Spiritual Emergence Syndrome and Kundalini—is not just here, and it is not just in our private practices. It is happening more and more every day. The people at Rutgers understood because they experience it. This is much bigger than we realize. There are two physicians here from Russia who are going to present their research. We have a researcher here from Australia and from several other countries, too, I understand. This is global and the more deeply we study this phenomena the more it gives hope and support for the goodness of humankind.

Five years ago I moved to Baltimore and started a private practice in breath and body work in which I work with this energy. I practice in association with several psychotherapists who refer clients who are adult survivors of incest or physical abuse, and who can't release the chronic stress in their bodies from their childhood. I also see clients who come to me specifically for Spiritual Emergence Syndrome or Kundalini arousal. (It's no accident that after becoming a respiratory therapist, I became a massage therapist.) Studying this energy in ancient texts or modern writings we read over and over of the relationship between breath, movement and

---

[9] I've heard this often in other talks given at the Kundalini Research Network Conference. The helping professions are ready to hear about spiritual awakenings, or what we call "Spiritual Emergence Syndrome." See the Appendix II on SEN and KRN.

touch. As a therapist I work with this energy all the time. It comes through me, not from me. Before I begin working with a patient I say a prayer, asking God and the Holy Spirit to help me get out of my own way, so the energy can come though. When I'm finished I say a prayer of thanks.[10]

My clients are releasing the chronic stress that they have carried around for decades. And I have a vehicle to share this love I received in my near-death experience. At the same time, clients are reporting symptoms and signs of this energy arousal and what we are calling Kundalini, or Spiritual Emergence Syndrome.

It doesn't matter how this energy is awakened: when close to death, in childbirth, during meditation or the many other ways we are going to hear about at this conference. What matters is that *it* is happening and with *it* comes a more loving and compassionate human being.

---

[10] By "Holy Spirit" here, I also include Kundalini. That energy connects to the higher energy known as Higher Power or God.

# THREE

# Life as a Practical Mystic

Practical Mystics:

- —Talk with God through prayer, listen to God through meditation.
- —Perceive God in nature and in the action of unconditional love.
- —Celebrate our connectedness to Divine Energy.
- —Have peace and joy in our daily life.
- —Love and honor ourselves and the Earth equally.
- —Celebrate our connectedness to our inner life.
- —Care and protect our True Self/Child Within.
- —Understand forgiveness as a heartfelt release.
- —Treat our physical body as sacred.
- —Enjoy being in our bodies.
- —Appreciate the *now* by thriving on direct experience.
- —Experience reverence and natural enjoyment in infinite variety.

—Are passionate and faithful in all our relationships.
—Need something bigger than we are to be awed by
   and to commit to.
—Are at our most powerful in compassionate service.
—Have humility.
—Have healthy boundaries and limits, yet
—Enjoy and thrive on boundlessness and unity.

A Mystic is someone who relates to God in direct experiential communion, through the soul or the Child Within. There is direct knowledge of reality, and most of our journey leads to this reality. If we can apply this relationship every day in our personal life, we will likely feel the presence of *Grace*.

Our journey of psychospiritual growth may peak in the experience of this communion. The challenge is to keep our feet planted firmly, to live in both worlds and bring the attributes of spirit here: to be an instrument of God while at the same time functioning here, taking care of ourselves and paying our bills. To achieve this balance, we can live by our own inner laws rather than outer pressures, to operate in this world but not be of it.[1] The above characteristics reflect my own experience and that of people I have known and assisted on their journey.

Practical Mystics have not been overtaken seriously by the material plane. We may enjoy playing in the material, but we want to go deeper. We care about ourselves and about our world and usually accept that there are no fixed answers, no real issues to fight for if it will hurt ourselves or others. There is only love to share. We have taken the energy from our mind and our gut and moved it to our hearts. We realize the difference. We know that this metaphor of the human heart is not only metaphor, it is real.

[1] The media will continue to feed us all the bad news, but we can live centered within ourselves, spirit and God.

We work with our hearts to complete our unfinished business with others and to stay current in all our relationships. A good example here is the real way we handle forgiveness.

## Forgiveness

Each act of forgiveness completes us. If, that is, we are ready to forgive. Because we love and honor our whole being, our heartfelt feelings as well as what our intellect tells us is right, forgiveness gives us as much time as we need to be ready for it. What is important is to honor what we feel, honor what is going on in our hearts. Some of us may be ready, may be in a comfortable place to forgive, and others may not. Practical Mystics can tell the difference in what we were taught to believe, and what we feel now and what we are ready for. We know what premature forgiveness feels like. If we say what we are not ready for, we can feel the lies in our heart. If we are hurt by someone, we need to feel our hurt to heal us. (See section on grieving, p 80.) By experiencing continuously what is real, we change, getting closer to ourselves and to Reality, with a capital R.

When our heart lets us know it is ready to open, we can ask for God's help. We can open to spirit, asking it to nourish us and help us create our healing through forgiveness.

Forgiveness can help us create the beginnings of a world where suffering is over, loss becomes impossible and anger makes no sense. The world can become a place of joy, abundance, charity and endless giving. "Forgiveness becomes the Light that it reflects."[2]

Some of the current feelings that emerge from our depths are reverence, gratitude, trust, wonderment, awe and unconditional love. Others may start using the word "radiance" to describe a quality in us that we are oblivious to. Committing ourselves to loving service may feel selfish because it benefits

---

[2] From *A Course in Miracles.*

us as much as others. We recognize in everything we do that the physical and the psychological are only half the picture. We incorporate our heart, feelings, soul and spirit to create wholeness. We know that what is nourishing emanates from spirit to this reality.

## Enjoying the Ordinary

We Mystics treasure our moments of *Grace*. Some of us live from one experience to the next. A few years ago, though, I realized that I was in need of becoming more practical. Finally, I gave in to the realization of being a Mystic. No more struggles with my rational side, but lots of struggles with the chop wood, carry water, ho-hum routines. How could I be a Mystic and be grounded in the world at the same time?

I was patient with myself. I practiced living in the now by *enjoying* washing the dishes and even singing as I scrubbed the bathroom. I took a class in small-business management and even kept my checkbook balanced. I felt joy when I was able to meet all my monthly bills. I became a *Practical* Mystic. "Impossible," my friends told me. "Practical Mystic is an oxymoron! It's self-contradictory and absurd!"

Absurd or not, as we awaken it's time to transform the contradiction and unite the opposites. This is because we who are awakening spiritually are coming out, bringing our spiritual connections to our work and personal lives. We are hospice workers, custodians, physicians, ecologists, therapists, teachers, CPAs, truck drivers, nurses, social workers, volunteers, counselors, waiters and waitresses, professors, cab drivers and more. We are moving into the political arena, because we stand up for what we believe. We are dedicated to the truth about how we feel and what we think and intuit. In every role that we live, we feel alive. We are deeply loyal to our spirituality. Our goals are to become instruments of Divine Energy and evolve so we may embrace and extend unconditional love.

## Enjoying Alone Time

We have learned much of our process by learning how to enjoy being alone. This is simply a state of mind that allows us to understand loving and honoring our selves. We can understand that our real journey is about self-discovery in relationship to God and others, about honoring our physical

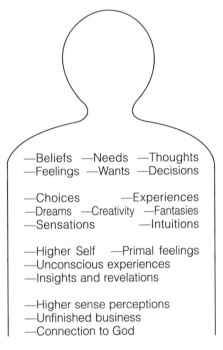

—Beliefs —Needs —Thoughts
—Feelings —Wants —Decisions

—Choices              —Experiences
—Dreams —Creativity —Fantasies
—Sensations          —Intuitions

—Higher Self —Primal feelings
—Unconscious experiences
—Insights and revelations

—Higher sense perceptions
—Unfinished business
—Connection to God

**My Inner Life**—It is important to become fully aware of what is coming up for us from moment to moment in our inner life, to observe our own heart and mind at work.

self and our inner life. We are not afraid of being intimate with ourselves, of being alone. Once we have developed silence and self-love through exploring our inner life, we can make this quality our standard for intimacy with someone else.

When we experience transformation fully, we will be tuned in and fully aware of our inner life all the time. We will then be easily able to access our intuition and creativity.

We are spiritual philanthropists. Because we have a spiritual connection that is infinitely bountiful, we love and seek to do good for our fellow humans. Our greatest need and joy is to share the heart connection with others, which keeps us in direct connection to our reality here and our reality with God. We have the ability to be totally absorbed in service, one hand extended to our brothers and sisters, while the other hand remains in God's.

We realize in this process that our power comes from releasing into the flow of Divine Energy. We have learned how to invite the higher energy in and how to let it help us release our personal feelings and thoughts, so we can be swept into the loving feelings of the higher current (see chapter 8). As we release into this higher harmony, we experience peace and joy while remaining citizens of planet Earth. Practicing the art of patience, we realize that the goal is reached while continuing the journey.

## Meditation

Modern biofeedback technology can take us through the first stages of meditation. These little devices are easily found in catalogues like Sharper Image, Damark, Radio Shack, etc. Tapes are available to teach meditation.

I used biofeedback technology, then after two or three weeks found I could slip into an altered state without help. I meditate lying on my bed without a pillow—my body knows pillows mean sleep—taking three or four slow cleansing breaths and then waiting for my mind to quiet. Sometimes it does and sometimes it chatters for 19 minutes and I have 30 seconds of peace. I identify the whole 20 minutes with my observer self. I watch my chattering monkey-mind and know it isn't who I am. My aches or negative feelings are not me. I am the one who watches and decides where to focus my awareness. After 20 to 30 minutes I come out of this state feeling rested and refreshed.

## A Practical Mystic's Story

Diane Mann had what she calls a very sad childhood in a family that had a great deal of trouble communicating. She told me that as a child she was extremely withdrawn, scared and depressed. As a teenager she became worse, was nearly unable to use a telephone, and remained shy and withdrawn in college. She had individual counseling and attended group therapy over the years, trying to get to the roots of her pain. She completed a master's degree in social work and was a psychiatric social worker for several years.

Her spiritual awakening happened when she was about 40 years old.

While visiting a friend in Washington State, I was driving alone in the hills near Mount St. Helens. I never liked being alone and avoided it. I stopped to take some pictures and ate lunch in a field of gladioli. I took pictures of the flowers with Mount St. Helens in the background. The colors of the flowers, the sky and the smells were amazing. I got back in the car feeling incredibly comfortable being alone, which was not like me at all. I drove three or four miles. I could see the Lewis River below surrounded by mountains and Mount St. Helens behind it. I gasped. For a moment I couldn't breathe.

I found another rest stop and watched people in the lake. I wanted to swim so much, but I had no bathing suit and was mad at myself for not bringing one. I decided just to sit and enjoy the scene anyway and then drove on three or four miles. Suddenly I knew I had to go back and swim. I felt a knowing from outside myself that let me know I had to go back. I realized there was this spirit or the Holy Ghost guiding me back. I had no doubt of its presence.

Time had shifted. Suddenly I was back at the lake and people who had been there were gone. I was alone, but I knew I wasn't alone. I parked the car and walked into the water up to my waist. I think it was a boat launch area because there was a Do Not Enter sign, but there was no one to stop me. I put my head back in the water three times, like they do in a baptism, all the while looking up at Mount St. Helens and crying. The crying was so cleansing. I knew what was going on and at the same time I was totally overwhelmed by the experience.

I walked back to the car and picked up the book I had brought along. Opening it, I knew I would turn to the exact page I needed. The book was called *The Spirit of Findhorn.* Still crying, I walked over to some trees and sat and read, "I am a child of God and I cannot settle for second best. I deserve to have the best, God's unconditional love . . ."

The experience is still here. I can draw on it anytime.

A while ago Diane gave up her administrative position as director of a social services agency and became a hospice social worker. She wanted direct contact with patients, especially the dying. When I asked her recently about the term "Practical Mystic," she laughed and said, "Yeah, I know. I often function on two levels with my patients. I'm sitting there with them, doing the financial stuff, figuring out how we're going to apply for financial help. But at the same time there's our eye contact. I'm tuning in to heart stuff, either touching their arm or shoulder, helping them to know it's okay to ask for help. Sometimes we become tearful together. I can't believe what I'm doing now. My patients tell me they love me, and now I can say it back. I don't understand completely any of this, but sometimes it just pours out. In any situation now, I can always think back to my experience at the lake and draw on it. It always guides me with my dying patients, and it even guides me to get what I deserve."

"I'm just now finding who I really am. I'm still a little scared to be alone and be with who I really am, but I'm finding out that it's okay. I've been too dependent my whole life on others to fill my needs or tell me what to do next. Now, I'm doing what I want. I love working with dying people and I love going out into nature whenever I can. I take walks. I get back in touch with God's Spirit."

Diane is not shy anymore either. Recently she coordinated and supervised housing for The New England IANDS Conference. She also has taken my place facilitating the IANDS support group at the University of Connecticut with Bruce Greyson.

## Unconditional Love

A prayer I say silently before every breath and body work session:[3]

> Dear God, dear Universe, please may I be an instrument of your healing energy, your unconditional love, your oneness and your wisdom. Please help me to get out of the way so you can come through.

And toward the end of every session:

> Thank you, God, for allowing me to be an instrument of your unconditional love and healing energy.

Aided by those two prayers I never try to move the energy where I think it should go. The energy has its own wisdom. Although it moves through me, it is not of me. If it originated with me, I would be exhausted after each session. Instead, I am peacefully energized. And I try to live my life in the same way.

Unconditional love is the feeling that is not only close to my heart, but is my heart—and my soul and my spirit and my reason for being here. Perhaps your reason for being here, too. Unconditional love is the action of God. It is the emotional component of the Divine Energy that is called Kundalini by Tantric Buddhists. It is the most powerful healing and creative energy in the Universe.

We felt unconditional love in our spiritual awakenings, and now as we do our own inner work it manifests again, only

---

[3] During the prayer I visualize the Pillar of Light described on page 156.

this time from our core, our Child Within. Its voice in our inner life and its actions in our outer life become stronger and stronger. We now transform false self/negative ego's voice and actions to assist us as positive ego.[4] Now our hearts and our souls are in charge. Our lives becomes an expression of our bond with God. As this happens we realize that our True Self/Child Within is unconditional love, and we become stronger instruments of God's love.

A law of the Universe becomes a solid law in our lives. *Everything we give out we get back.* When we contained pain and negativity from the past, we projected that darkness onto others, and we received darkness back. Now as we approach wholeness, we can see our love reaching out and lighting our way, lighting the faces of our loved ones. And the Light comes back to us again. We learn as we awaken spiritually that the Universe is benevolent and purposeful. As we express unconditional love, that benevolence surrounds us.

But there are certain conditions that go with this blessing. Since unconditional love is flowing acceptance on an emotional level, the only way to extend unconditional love is first to heal oneself emotionally. We can't heal others, only ourselves—and then extend that love, no strings attached. Unconditional love transcends subject-object relationships. We learn to accept the world, trust the process, see ourselves in everyone and everyone in us. We feel compassion for others, knowing we can't change them. We can empathize with their pain, but we don't have to feel it. And we don't try to fix them. *The way I can help is to be my True Self and lovingly maintain my own center with humility. I can live my life in a way that gives the people I love a choice.*

I felt unconditional love for the first time from my grandmother during my NDE. And then with God. There is no way to explain the intensity of that Divine Energy. After the experiences an invitation to return lingered, to come to God in an

---

[4] See Whitfield's *Healing The Child Within.*

intimate relationship of love. That love is expressed when I extend that love to others. When I act in service, there is a never-ending supply because God is always holding one of my hands and I am extending the other. Because I love myself, I am careful and protective of this relationship I have with God and my True Self/Child Within.

Later I will discuss long-term, intimate relationships that utilize the emotional component of unconditional love as Divine Energy. In all relationships, unconditional love is and must always be a free gift.

Practical Mystics have healed or are healing their inner life or Child Within and are content to stay in that healing state, sensing that our natural vocation is to be an agent of healing, to embody health, and to incarnate passion and compassion for life. Our greatest reward is to be in and give unconditional love.

And we don't just look up to God. We look within and around!

# F O U R
# Spiritual and Value Changes

The growing body of literature on the aftereffects of spiritual awakening shows consistently that experiencers undergo a greater appreciation for life, self-acceptance, a heightened sense of purpose and self-understanding, a desire to learn, elevated spirituality, greater ecological and planetary concern, heightened intuition to the point of being psychic (see chapter 8) and concern for others. Psychophysical changes include increased physical sensitivity; a higher sensitivity to light and sound, alcohol and drugs; a feeling that our brains have been altered to encompass more; and a feeling that we are now using our whole brain rather than just part of it (see chapter 7).

The 1985 research project Bruce Greyson and I did with individuals who had attempted suicide showed that the psychological aftereffects of the near-death

55

experience eliminate further thoughts of suicide. Suicide attempters know that they still have the same problems after experiencing an NDE, but they now have a much larger framework for the meaning of life, and a healthier perspective toward themselves and their world view. Suicide attempters who didn't have an NDE, who were given books to read about the near-death experience, developed some of the same positive aftereffects and attitudes.

A spiritual awakening causes paradoxical changes in attitude in that it romanticizes death, but it also romanticizes life. Experiencers say their experiences are not about death but about life. Before their experience, they felt they were only existing. Now they feel really alive. These changes require different values, attitudes, interests, and a greater appreciation for commonplace features of life. This includes increased spirituality and concern for others, and decreased materialism, competitiveness and fear of death. Emotional changes include suddenly being in touch with our feelings.

Sometimes people who were unprepared to face the changes brought about by awakening spiritually have doubted their sanity. Unfortunately, the feedback they got from mental health professionals when they described their experiences and aftereffects was negative. This invalidation and rejection of their experience discouraged them from seeking help to understand their experience and changes. When I told a psychiatrist about my NDE, as I related earlier, he didn't understand and prescribed antidepressants. I wasn't depressed. I *did* feel confused and overwhelmed, but not depressed. In my experience I had awakened memories of emotionally loaded scenes and I didn't know what to do with my strong feelings. From the doctor's response, I concluded that no one could understand, so I stopped talking or seeking help.[1]

---

[1] The attitude of the health care profession is changing rapidly to include or at least respect these experiences. If you seek therapy and the therapist doesn't understand—seek other help.

## Out of the Closet

People are talking more commonly and openly about their near-death experiences, possibly because of the growing media attention, reading new books or attending support groups. One woman described her NDE as a great tapestry. She realized that all her life she was seeing it only from the back, where the colors were dull and the weaving flat. Her NDE reversed the tapestry so that now everything had texture and more intense color. Her experience happened as she was surrendering to a terminal disease. After her awakening she had a spontaneous remission, and she says her life and the way she views it have improved tremendously. The last time I talked with her, she was running a center for senior citizens, something she would never have considered before.

Howard Storm, former chairman of the Art Department at the University of Kentucky, served on a panel with myself and two other NDErs at the 1990 IANDS conference in Washington, D.C. He described himself before his NDE as "an egocentric, self-centered atheist." He emerged from his experience, which contained a painful life review where he witnessed his journey from a loving child to a cynical adult, a changed man. He plans to go into full-time ministry work. All of this was difficult for his wife, who said that "her husband died . . . and came back a stranger."

Joe Geraci, another experiencer, had an NDE in 1977, about a week after surgery. He had already been discharged from the hospital and started hemorrhaging at home. His wife Joan, a nurse, rushed him to the emergency room. While lying on a stretcher he looked up at her and said, "Good-bye, Joan. I'm going to die." Instantly, he was in the Light. He emerged from his experience with an incredible feeling of warmth and love and says that words can't describe what it was. His subsequent life changes characterize his experience better than words: "I used to hunt. I can't hunt anymore. I just can't. I couldn't watch TV for a long time after my NDE because of all the violence. I used to be a policeman. I can't do that anymore. Not taking away from policemen and their lot. Lord knows I know what it is and God bless them for doing it, but I couldn't do it anymore. I wouldn't last ten minutes on the street."

Steve Price had his NDE in Vietnam. During a battle he was hit in the chest by two pieces of hot flying metal. He was assaulted by intense pain, his lung collapsed and he lost consciousness. He told me: "I saw everything that had happened in my life. I saw myself as a baby, I saw the things my father did to me, and I saw a lot of things I really didn't want to remember . . ." He saw all the physical and emotional abuse he had received as a child as young as two. He also saw himself at age seven or eight stealing $20 from his grandfather. Then he was aware that he was lying wounded and dying on a battlefield in Vietnam, feeling guilt and shame over money he had stolen when he was a child. "At that point I hated myself. I knew I wasn't dead but I kept seeing these pictures of my life in my mind and I thought I was about to die. I felt relieved when the life review ended, totally relieved, the way a child is relieved when he gets a spanking and it suddenly ends."

A few days later, after he was flown to Clark Air Force Base in the Philippines, he was lying on a stretcher waiting to be rolled into surgery when the brick wall next to him turned into the Light. He left his body behind and went into the Light. Soon he was outdoors near a stream and met with his dead grandfather. He wanted to cross the stream and knew if he did he could never return to his body. His grandfather told him to return, that he couldn't stay, and then he was back in his body.

I asked him if his life changed. "I felt myself changing almost against my will. I tried to halt the transformation by going back to 'Nam to continue fighting. But once I arrived there I found I couldn't. It's like I said in the IANDS support group, I really didn't know if I had killed anybody the first time I was there. I really don't know. But the second time, I knew I didn't. I couldn't do it if I had to. Even today I couldn't do it if I was backed into a corner. I went through maybe ten years of resisting these changes and then I found Ray Moody's first book, *Life After Life,* and I took a class on Death and Dying. Then it started hitting me, all the memories, and I knew I couldn't resist anymore. And the biggest thing is I became more compassionate. I didn't care about material things as I had before. I wanted to help people."

It took Steven several support group meetings to realize that his grandfather didn't send him back to punish him. He felt so guilty about seeing himself stealing $20 when he was a child that he assumed his grandfather wouldn't let him stay because of that. Finally Steve realized, "He sent me back because he loves me. I've walked around for 22 years thinking he was punishing me, when he sent me back because he loves me!"

Another Vietnam vet told researcher Robert Sullivan about his experience following a helicopter crash. "It was peaceful and cool. I could see others like myself just sort of floating around only inches off the ground, dead. Our eyes met. They are like me, only they are Vietcong; but there are no hard feelings between us, just something we have in common." One can only begin to imagine the ramifications of change from experiencing "the enemy" in this way.

## What's Real

The first change that almost all experiencers have in common is that we are not afraid to die. The next change we talk about is how we now feel about others. We care more, have greater compassion and feel love for everyone. At the same time, our drive for material success decreases—often to the dismay of others. And life becomes more precious: it's as though we have taken a piece of the Light and brought it back with us and now we want and need to share it with others. *And the more we give it away, the more we have to give.*

Those changes cause another big change for experiencers: risk-taking becomes easier. We have demonstrated statistically in the research that almost immediately, again to the dismay of close others, people who have had a spiritual awakening are able to take risks more easily, especially if the risk involves helping another.

Sharon Grant, whose NDE is described in *Full Circle*, says, "It took a long time to deal with it, to integrate it and to learn about what I'm supposed to be. You learn what we're really supposed to be doing on this Earth, how we're really supposed to relate to each other.

"Every day I chop wood and carry water. It's still an ordinary life but the important thing is to give some of that peace, completeness and love you get from the NDE to whomever comes into your life. That includes the people you work with, the people at the grocery store, the child you smile at and the dog that you reach down to pet."

So our spiritual needs are taken care of by sharing the Light of unconditional love with others. We are renewed by this sharing. We are also renewed by walking in the woods, sitting at the shore and watching the sun come up or go down. Anything in nature is now renewing and sacred. We see God in all things great and small. I'll talk more about this kind of seeing later.

## Spirituality and Religion

These kinds of spiritual changes aren't about any one religion, but embrace and expand all religions. This feels universal. It seems that by embracing everybody's beliefs, or just by embracing everybody, we are breaking down differences by seeing similarities. There is a sense that all religions have beauty and all have truth and we feel at home in any. We believe in the transcendent unity of all religions. We feel no need to organize a new religion or cult. There are no leaders in this movement and no need for anyone to take control.[2] As Joseph Campbell said, "Underneath the Masks of God, there is only God!"

## Conclusion

Researchers all over the world have heard and recounted the same results I have reported here. To our great delight, the researchers themselves now report the same value changes in their lives, too. It is as though by working closely with this material and this source, they gain many of the same changes. It is realistic to say that interest in spiritual growth nurtures the seed of awakening and propels anyone who desires it onto this journey of self-discovery and enlightenment.

---

[2] Authentic spirituality is universal and embraces all. It is about opening to Love. Occasionally groups form that try to restrict spirituality or to define rigid parameters around the experiences. Such a group might be a cult, or at the very least antithetical to the kind of spirituality we are describing. Should you encounter such a group, you can easily walk away from its destructive influence.

# FIVE

# Kundalini Energy and How It Works

W hat changes us in a spiritual awakening? One thing to consider is that we may have had a powerful energy force activated within us. One name that has been given to that energy is Kundalini. Scientists from the Kundalini Research Network (KRN) have begun to define Kundalini as "the evolutionary energy/consciousness force. . . . [Its] awakening affects a transformative process in the psycho-physiological and spiritual realms and results, ultimately, in the realization of the oneness of the individual and universal consciousness."

Transpersonal psychotherapist Bonnie Greenwell, physicist Paul Pond and others of KRN[1] hypothesize that Kundalini is associated with and may be the cause of mystical experiences, psychic ability, creativity and

---

[1] Including physicians Evon Kason, Bruce Greyson, Robert Turner and Lee Sannella.

genius. Some observers note that Kundalini may be linked to some forms of mental illness. One of KRN's goals to is make Kundalini known to the Western world, especially the scientific and medical communities, therapists, health care workers and those who have had Kundalini experiences but may not realize it.

Phenomena associated with the rising or arousal of Kundalini energy is occurring with increasing frequency to Westerners who have never heard of it and have done nothing consciously to arouse it. The term "rising" is often used in this way to describe the arousal of the Kundalini energy to an undetermined level that may or may not complete itself as a sustained evolution of consciousness. Felt as vast rushes of energy through the body, Kundalini-rising can create profound changes in the structure of people's physical, mental, emotional and spiritual lives.

## Western Research

Bonnie Greenwell addressed some of the problems and joys of Kundalini-rising in her doctoral dissertation, which she has published as *Energies of Transformation: A Guide to the Kundalini Process.* This book summarizes her six years of research and experience working with individuals who have awakened Kundalini.

> After centuries of hiding in nearly every culture on the globe under the guise of a secret esoteric truth, the Kundalini experience is reported more and more frequently among modern spiritual seekers, and it appears to be occurring even among people who are not pursuing disciplined or esoteric spiritual practices. When this happens to those who have no understanding of the profound correlations between the physical and mystical experiences, it can leave them bewildered and frightened, even psychologically fragmented. When they turn to traditional physicians, psychotherapists or church advisors, their anxiety is compounded by the general

lack of understanding in Western culture regarding the potentiality in the human psyche for profound spiritual emergence and its relationship to energy.[2]

How Kundalini manifests itself in experiencers is called the physio-Kundalini syndrome.[3] Researcher Bruce Greyson did a scientific study of the physio-Kundalini hypothesis. He reported those results at the 1992 KRN conference.

> As a group, near-death experiencers reported experiencing almost twice as many physio-Kundalini items as did people who had close brushes with death but no NDE, and people who had never come close to death.
>
> As a check on whether the physio-Kundalini questionnaire might be measuring nonspecific strange experiences, I threw into the analysis the responses of a group of hospitalized psychiatric patients. They reported the same number of physio-Kundalini [index] items as did the non-NDE control group. There were two unexpected and ambiguous "control" groups in my studies: people who claimed to have had NDEs but described experiences with virtually no typical NDE features; and people who denied having had NDEs but then went on to describe prototypical near-death experiences. In their responses to the physio-Kundalini questionnaire, the group that made unsupported claims of NDEs were comparable to the non-NDE control group, while the group that denied having NDEs (but according to their responses on the NDE scale, did) were comparable to the group of NDErs. In regard to awakening Kundalini, then, having an experience mattered, but thinking you had one didn't.

## Manifestations

Because Western medicine does not acknowledge the East's physio-Kundalini model, symptoms of Kundalini

---

[2] From *Energies of Transformation: A Guide to the Kundalini Process.*

[3] Bentov, Sannella, and Greyson 1992.

arousal are often diagnosed as physical and/or psychological problems that fit within the Western allopathic diagnostic categories. For example, the shaking, twisting and vibrating so well known to experiencers could be diagnosed as a neurological disorder. It is also hard to recognize the energy presence because it manifests itself in so many different patterns. Because its symptoms mimic so many disorders of the mind and body, even people familiar with the Kundalini concept are unsure whether they are witnessing rising Kundalini energy or distresses of the mind and body. The danger is in accepting prescriptions for drugs that Western physicians give to alleviate symptoms and possibly stopping the continuation of this natural healing mechanism. Any symptoms that can be alleviated by using the Kundalini model should not be treated and suppressed with drugs.

In studying the manifestations that Kundalini arousal may take, Greyson compiled a questionnaire entitled *The Physio-Kundalini Syndrome Index,* containing 19 manifestations in three categories.

Motor manifestations
—Spontaneous body movements
—Strange posturing
—Breath changes
—Body locking in certain positions

Sensory manifestations
—Spontaneous tingling or vibrations
—Orgasmic sensations
—Progression of physical sensations up the legs and back and over the head
—Extreme heat or cold (in isolated areas of the body)
—Pain that comes and goes abruptly
—Internal lights or colors that light up the body (or are seen internally)
—Internal voices (and internal whistling, hissing or roaring noises)

Psychological manifestations
  —Sudden bliss or ecstasy for no reason
  —Sudden anxiety or depression for no reason
  —Speeding or slowing of thoughts
  —Expanding beyond the body
  —Watching the body from a distance

Kenneth Ring and Christopher Rosing reported almost identical results as Greyson's in their latest research, *The Omega Project:* "Near-death experiencers reported experiencing almost twice as many physio-Kundalini items as did people who had close brushes with death but no NDE, and people who had never come close to death."[4]

## The Concept of Energy

Kundalini is a natural phenomenon with intense psychological and physical effects that can catapult a person into a higher state of consciousness. This analysis is based on the reality that we are extensive fields of consciousness as well as biological beings. As fields of consciousness, we have a spirit-body made of various energy systems. Various experiences can manifest in the energy or spirit body. These can be highly emotional and are usually connected to activities in the autonomic nervous system and the hormonal and muscular systems of the physical body. These experiences can be repressed in our memories but are manifested as stress in our energy/spirit/biological body. Felt as "blocks in our energy," they can be released emotionally and physically.[5] Thus, Kundalini is fueled by emotion and helps us to release a lifetime of buried stress, resulting in a physically, emotionally, mentally and spiritually more healthy person.

---

[4] Ring and Rosing. "The Omega Project," *The Journal of Near-Death Studies,* 1990.
[5] Working with Kundalini energy and specifically by balancing the chakra system, alternative therapies suggested in this book can do more to alleviate these unwanted sensations than Western allopathic medicine has shown.

Whether this energy is called Chi, Ki, prana, Kundalini, bioenergy, Holy Spirit, vital force or simply energy, the assumptions about it are similar. Several healing aids use a concept of releasing this stored energy: Shiatsu, polarity, acupuncture, acupressure, Reikian body work, bioenergy integration, holotropic integration, T'ai Chi and some forms of massage. In discussing an energy model, there is a common limitation set up by the tendency to concretize the energy, to make it tangible, to view it as physical stuff with physical properties. The concept of energy in the human body, and any form of life, is best understood as dynamic, a verb not a noun. There is no such thing as energy in physical form. Rather, there is activity described in energetic terms.

So when we speak of life energy, we characterize activity, not a measurable physical entity. According to the Chinese explanation, energy is like the wind, invisible but with visible effects such as waves on a pond stirred by a breeze. The concept of energy is a useful way of describing the deeper hidden patterns and processes that underlie the more visible effects. The results of the energy, the visible waves on the pond, can be seen in the lives that we lead, the love that we share and the selfless service that we extend. Or as the Bible puts it, "By their fruits you shall know them." (Matthew 7:20.)

This invisible energy appears to be a deep, hidden pattern or process of integration that unifies all of our dimensions, physical, mental, emotional and spiritual. We could also call it the creative intelligence that is working to make us whole.[6]

My first encounters with Kundalini energy were intense. Over the years they have tapered off to gentle, subtle and infrequent. Here's an example of a joyful experience:

I'd take my daily four-mile walk in the hot Florida sunshine. Often, I came back feeling euphoric and swam or showered and then meditated. Sometimes I perceived

---

6 This information comes from an editorial I wrote for The *Journal of Near-Death Studies* (13:2, Winter 94) entitled "Kundalini and Healing in the West."

tingling sensations moving up my back and feel myself surrounded in Light. I became acutely aware of the love that
connects and is all living things. Sometimes, I felt sweet currents like honey flowing downward in my head, behind my
face. I felt my hands expand and then my very being went
out into It. I chuckled inside over my feeling of bliss and I
heard the chuckle echo and rebound through the Universe.
On the days that happened, I perceived the energy fields
around everything.

## Chakras–Energy Centers of Transformation

Chakra is Sanskrit for wheel and describes energy centers
or transducers that convey energy from one dimension into
another. In this case the energy is conveyed from our environment to our energy body to our physical body, or in
reverse—from our inner life to our awareness (if we are
awake or conscious of our inner life) and then out to our
environment. There are seven major chakras, and many more
minor ones, contained in our subtle energy body that interact with our physical body. Each can be visualized as a center where many of the streams of energy—nadis or
meridians—come together through the human body. *Each
chakra mediates a different level of consciousness with the
outer environment.*

This system works for our growth and healing potential.
Chakras modulate discrete frequencies that represent every
variety of human experience on the mental, emotional, physical and spiritual levels. A pain in our hearts, a bright idea, a
gut feeling, a tingling up our spines are all feelings originat-
ing in the vortex of a chakra energy center. So are experiences of oneness, sexual desire, self-pity, a beautiful singing
voice and even addictions.[7] A lump in our throat, butterflies

---

[7] From a workshop and unpublished book by Gloria St. John, *A Journey
Throughout the Chakras*. For further information see bibliography.

in our stomach, pressure in our heads—all originate from a chakra picking up our inner life or perceiving the outer environment, then broadcasting it to us through our physical system until we feel it can focus on it.

After a spiritual awakening, many of us want to stay in the higher chakras, the higher spiritual levels, and not deal with the lower three. However, we need the balance of all seven.

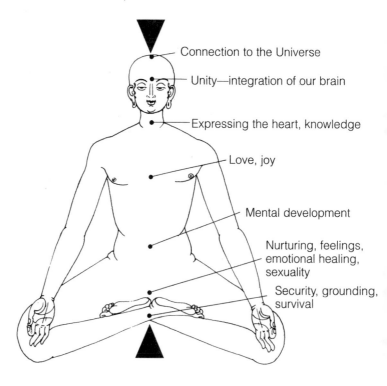

Connection to the Universe

Unity—integration of our brain

Expressing the heart, knowledge

Love, joy

Mental development

Nurturing, feelings, emotional healing, sexuality

Security, grounding, survival

Beginning at the bottom, the first chakra is located at the base of the spine and opens down toward the ground. It keeps us alive in the body and draws sustenance from the soul or True Self. It is our sense of grounding, our work of survival on the planet. When working properly it is our sense of security. An imbalance brings on fear.

When we talk about getting grounded we mean staying with issues of this reality, coming back to practical issues and common sense. Experiencers and spiritual seekers in general have a tendency to intellectualize and fantasize, or go into their heads and indulge in wishful or magical thinking. A great many New Age concerns can turn into escapist delusions. This danger can be averted by solid grounding—getting down to basics, or first chakra issues.

The problem of staying grounded comes up over and over again at support group meetings and research conferences. If you need grounding, it's advisable to stop reading books on Kundalini for a while.[8] Put yourself with safe friends who are grounded, take a barefoot walk outdoors—if possible, hug a tree or lie down on the earth. Adjust your diet to foods that are grounding, like meats, root vegetables such as potatoes and carrots—and the favorite standard among researchers and experiencers, fast-food french fries! The salt and grease will bring you down immediately. We also agree that during these periods you should meditate and practice yoga less.

Grounding requires the willingness, honesty and courage to face ourselves as we are and our world as it is—no distance, no exclusions, no avoidances, no anesthesia. *When we are solidly grounded our heart chakra can function openly because our first chakra is balancing it.*

The second chakra is approximately two inches below the navel. If it is healthy and well-balanced, the second chakra is responsible for fluid actions and nurturing, being able to accept our own feelings and tolerate others. We feel at home in the world. If damage was done to this chakra in

---

[8] I caution against reading Kundalini literature during emotional turbulence because it can promote more energy flow, or awareness of energy flow into your body. Your false self and True Self struggle for control, and focusing on Kundalini energy, or using it to distract can lead to ego inflation. Stay grounded. The waters are rough enough without making them rougher for yourself.

childhood or if it is out of balance now for some other reason, there is a sense of separation, abandonment, rejection, anger, rage, fear of loss, etc. Many teachers believe that this is the chakra of emotional healing, going back to very early childhood development. The second chakra is also the seat of our sexuality.

The third chakra is called the solar plexus and is at the level of the diaphragm. It includes the realms of social interaction, education, mental development and career. It equips us to interact effectively with the fundamentals of the external world. The virtues of justice, fairness and equality, and the institutions of law, politics and education develop from the third chakra. Feeling hungry or empty is also a third chakra expression.[9]

As I said above, avoiding these first three chakras is another way of attempting spiritual bypass or high-level denial. Since we need to live in the physical world, we will achieve harmony and balance only by embracing these three levels of consciousness defined by chakra one, two and three. Not to embrace them invites dis-ease and disharmony and imbalance.

During a spiritual awakening, our partially dormant and often totally shut down upper four chakras may be aroused or opened. Anyone pursuing psychospiritual growth will, over time, open these chakras. If we are aware of this and encourage these openings by doing our emotional work—dealing with our unfinished business—we will know when our consciousness level is shifting from one chakra to another.

The fourth chakra is located at heart level and relates to our capacity to love, to open up our hearts and to give. When this chakra is blocked a person may appear to be cold or inhibited, or may exhibit passivity in his or her life. This chakra governs joyfulness and is the master control center for

---

[9] From Gloria St. John's workshop.

regulating the emotions. Many, if not most, NDErs that Bruce Greyson, Ken Ring and I interviewed appeared to have had a heart chakra opening. You can tell by a vivid description of love—what we thought it was before and especially what we know it is now. In the classic *A Christmas Carol*, Scrooge's transformation at the end of the story is an excellent example of a heart chakra opening.

We have heard of a few cases where relatives have taken experiencers to court because of the aftereffects of a sudden heart chakra opening. Like Scrooge, these new experiencers want to give away their possessions. I will discuss more about caution in the next chapter under the sub-heading "Romantic Projection" (p. 83). I don't mean to be a wet blanket on expressions of the heart; expressing my heart and extending myself on the heart level is my reason for living. It is the way I live, but I need to caution that heart openings without healthy grounding can backfire and we can hurt ourselves, our families and unsuspecting others.

The fifth chakra is located in the throat and is a synthesis of head and heart energy. Those who have opened this center are able to *express* their heart experience of being alive. We are standing in the Light of our own soul. We are truly in a relationship with ourselves and the Universe.

The sixth chakra is between our eyebrows and often is called the third eye. Its opening is a direct result of spiritual practice. Meditation, selfless service and compassion are its prerequisite. From this opening there is a realization of unity, a marriage of opposites, the blending of male and female, mind and emotion, resistance and flow. In our inner life we discover our soul flame's identity and fall madly in love with our self.[10] It used to be that the closer we got to God, the more paradox there was in our lives. Now we move closer to

---

[10] By "soul flame's identity" I mean that we find contained inside our core that perfect mate we've been looking for. That's when we fall madly in love with our self. This is experiential and emerges as our false self dissipates.

God and at the same time confusion and paradox dissolves. In more grounded terms, this means a synthesis between both sides of our brain (see chapter 7), which then births a higher wisdom and creativity.

The seventh chakra at the top of the head funnels unlimited spiritual energy in and draws energy up from the lower centers in the process we know as enlightenment. We do not pray; we are prayer. We are no longer doing, just being. We have become our Higher Self.[11]

## A Word of Caution

This map of consciousness mediated through our energy body has been studied in great depth by ancient scholars and scientists in the East. There have been no easy translations yet to give Westerners a clear grasp of how Kundalini energy and the chakra system can work in our lives when we are so embedded in Western culture. Our best guide to all of this is our personal inner voice. As we travel our individual journeys, our inner life will become clearer and that subtle voice stronger. Read and learn from all available teachers and guides, but keep only the knowledge and information that rings true for you. Throw away the rest (see chapter 8).

## Ego Inflation

The experiencers with Kundalini symptoms who contacted Bruce Greyson and me often were scared, concerned, and wanted to know more. Some wanted to help with the research and occasionally claimed to be authorities. Some claimed that their Kundalini arousal had transformed them into gurus.

Probably the biggest problem at this early stage of understanding is ego inflation. Many who have read the Eastern

---

[11] St. John. op. cit.

literature identify strongly with the gurus. Eventually we pass through this stage, realizing that we are Westerners and that it's hard to translate these Eastern metaphors when our cultural roots are so completely different. Our reward for getting through ego inflation is humility, which is the solid foundation of a truly spiritual, healthy and whole human being. Some don't experience ego inflation and others get stuck in it.

Humility is the willingness to continue learning our whole lives. Being humble is that state of being open to experiencing and learning about self, others and God.[12] In this openness we are free to avoid the pitfalls of ego inflation and to connect with God again here in this reality. In this state of humility and second innocence, we can experience whatever comes.

## Spiritual Bypass

If we try to ignore our pain and achieve the higher levels of our consciousness, something, usually our false self/negative ego or shadow self, will hold us back until we work through our particular unfinished business. Trying to bypass the work that needs to be done on our negative ego/shadow backfires. This is called spiritual bypass, premature transcendence or high-level denial.[13] Spiritual bypass can be seen in any number of situations, from being born again in the fundamentalist sense, to focusing only on the Light, to becoming attached to a guru or technique. The consequences often are denial of the richness and healthy spontaneity of our inner life: trying to control oneself or others; all-or-none thinking and behaving; feelings of fear, shame and confusion; high tolerance for inappropriate behavior; frustration, addictions and compulsions; and unnecessary pain and suffering.[14]

---

[12] Whitfield, *Spirituality and Recovery,* 1985.

[13] Whitfield, *Co-Dependence*, 1991. Small, *Awakening in Time*, 1991.

[14] This is a compilation of C. Whitfield's ideas.

Recently I heard two glaring examples of spiritual bypass. First, a prison counselor complained of inmates who carried Bibles everywhere and refused rehabilitation because they had been so-called "born again." They are classic examples of high-level denial. Second, a family therapist had been treating a severely dysfunctional family in which the father was an alcoholic and sexual offender. He had molested all of his daughters and, as soon as that was revealed, claimed instant healing in a spiritual experience. He joined a fundamentalist church whose minister did the family a terrible disservice by supporting the "spiritual awakening" of this charming and persuasive talker, claiming the father no longer needed to feel guilt or remorse.

While at first glance these seem to be extreme examples, many of us know someone who has never done any inner work and is making everyone around them crazy with constant Bible quoting or by extolling some definitive path. When I see someone pushing an exclusive, restrictive system, I become cautious. Spiritual awakenings are universal, *include everyone* and exclude no one. They include all beliefs, are anti nothing, require no allegiance and embrace all.

S I X

# Freeing Blocked Energy

In Eastern traditions, Kundalini ideally would be awakened at an appropriate time by a guru who could properly guide in the development of that energy. A big part
of that guidance involves psychospiritual growth and is
nurtured along by the guru when energy blocks occur.
The guru assists the release of the blocks, which are
metaphoric as well as psycho-physiological.

Here in the West we have psychological and emotional parallels to release the same blocks. We can feel
energy blocks in our own body as a sensation of heat
radiation, vibration, burning pain or numbness.[1] It's

---

[1] Some Kundalini experts argue whether this is a true Kundalini energy block or simply "prana," life-force energy. As a body-based therapist I believe that what it is called isn't important,. What matters is the
pain is released and some healing occurs. Many times at the next
session, clients will report feeling the energy easily moving through

easier to explain blocks manifesting on the physical level, but they also exist on corresponding unconscious emotional and mental levels. When Kundalini energy is awakened and rises, its progression can be impeded by these energy blocks. The blocked areas can be painful until the block is removed. A block can involve many unpleasant feelings, issues, memories, images, symbolic processes and/or psychosomatic sensations. Enough sensations are experienced at a given area and in a repetitive way that eventually the energy block is released and the energy can discharge and dissipate.

Eastern traditions see all matter as composed of energy.[2] They view the human body as being composed of braided streams of moving energy called nadis—some writings say 720,000 and others up to 7,200,000. The Chinese discovered larger streams of energy through our body that they call meridians. When we became aware of the energy, we can feel these energy streams that are blocked or constricted. The burning can be felt on the physical level. It can be moved through and dissolved by breath and body work, acupuncture, acupressure, Shiatsu, polarity therapy, yoga and other aids. It may then either simultaneously or soon thereafter appear as symbols in consciousness, or dream states—unconscious level. Finally, understanding—the mental level—will happen either through self-contemplation or psychotherapy. All three levels can reveal themselves rapidly, one after the other, or unfold in a day or two (generally it is not much longer than that). There is usually a sense of revelation and catharsis.

These energy blocks can also be thought of as repressed emotion. If not removed, later in life they can manifest on the physical level as disease. If the energy is freed completely of blocks and painful impressions, it connects to the

---

where there had been pain before. They may report visualizing a flowing energy in colors, or Kundalini symbols, either during meditations, dreams or the breath and body work session.

[2] So does Western physics, but the knowledge hasn't been absorbed into the mainstream yet.

source of Universal energy, opening us to more transcendental experiences in consciousness and to this unlimited resource to help other people heal.

## Case Study

A 37-year-old woman with a history of spiritual awakening and subsequent Kundalini manifestations complains of pain on the upper left side of her neck, near the hairline. Face down on the massage table, she focuses on slow deep breathing. After gentle massage to the neck, shoulders and upper back, acupressure is applied. There are painful "blocks" that were not felt until now on the left side of the spine at about the T4 level (mid-shoulder blades). These are treated with acupressure and, more specifically, Shiatsu technique, and then cross-fiber massage.[3] Then energy balancing of the chakras is done. On a subtle level, her energy is balanced and she experiences a sense of peace and immediate relief of her neck pain.

Later in the session, while gently massaging her head, she starts to cry and says she misses her deceased grandmother. That night, in her dreams, she remembers a conflict between her grandmother and father when she was a small child. In psychotherapy the next day, she remembers and talks through buried anger with her father over this scene. Now, thirty-some years later, after experiencing the anger and sadness she is able to let go of it. Later, she says that she is free of neck pain.

These blocks were created in childhood by physical and/or emotional trauma. Children who aren't allowed to express their feelings about traumatic events repress the feelings, and on a subtle energy level they become a block. These blocks of repressed emotional energy wait there with a shell around them, forgotten, until later in life when in one

---

[3] Acupressure and Shiatsu focus on moving and rebalancing the energy and dissolving blocks. Cross fiber is the only form of therapeutic massage that brings in oxygenated arterial blood. Slow, deep, conscious breathing is important during this therapy.

way or another the energy is aroused and we start to do our inner work to become whole. Unless we become aware of these blocks, they limit us. Once we dissolve them, we free the energy flow to help us become healthier.

Because this woman did her inner work her heart was able to open more to her father and herself through authentic letting go. She released physical pain. Subsequently, in a dream, she remembered an ungrieved trauma and emotionally released that, too. Then she talked about it in therapy and was able to understand the repressed material and forgive her father. Many times people decide to forgive everyone and live in unconditional love without doing this vitally important inner life work, which is a form of spiritual bypass. My client is doing some hard inner work bravely and patiently and is beginning to love *herself* in the process.

## Grieving

Most blocks that are felt in the Physio-Kundalini Syndrome experience have to do with ungrieved losses. When the blocks are released on a physical level, posture improves as muscles release tension and align properly. On an emotional level, there is a need to *move through sadness.* Until recently our society has not honored our need to move through sadness or do grief work. Our society has labeled and frozen these feelings of loss or sadness as depression, and given us antidepressants to medicate us and move us away from the painful feelings without processing them and letting the feelings go in a natural way.[4] Other societies support the grieving process. We are beginning to support grief work, too, through the teachings of Elizabeth Kübler-Ross, Steven Levine and many others. This is a poem I wrote when learning to grieve.

---

[4] Don't stop taking any prescription drug for a physical disease or proven imbalance that has been diagnosed properly and is being managed by a physician, in exchange for doing grief work. If there is any question, find a consulting physician who is educated in both schools of thought.

## Good Grief

I.  Stop the world
    I need to get off.
    Feeling a squeeze
    Somewhere in my being.

II. Stop the world!
    And my monkey brain
       chatter!
    For all that was
    And never will be.

III. Stop my head
     And this thing called
        "Logic-"
     Get to the right
     And "braille"
        This whole thing.

IV. Give up some smiles
    And the stress behind
       them.
    Alleviate Grief
       By jumping in
          And being it.

Learning to grieve is crucial. When we grieve our ungrieved hurts, losses or traumas to completion, we get free of their chronic painful hold on us. A major part of the transformational journey is about letting go of past hurts that are blocking us. We can work through our grief in three relationships: (1) alone, and learn more about who we are; (2) with safe others in therapy and/or safe friends or family; (3) in relationship to God. Knowing God since our spiritual awakenings gives us the gift of moving through this journey more easily. We can ask God for help. When I realized that all I had to do was ask, I learned the true meaning of Higher Power.

Grieving unlocks and releases painful and destructive emotions. As we work through grief we learn progressively more about each of our feelings as they come up for us. Once we have grieved these losses to completion, we are free to be our True Self and to grieve any current hurts, losses or traumas as they may occur, so that we tend not to become stuck in them as we did in the past.[5]

After my father's death, grieving revealed more to me about my inner life. Once the shock of his sudden death subsided,

---

[5] Whitfield, 1987-95.

between bouts of tears I realized a heightened sense of this reality. This is an altered state that John Welwood calls "unconditional presence." He says that when the heart breaks out of its shell, we feel raw and vulnerable. This is the beginning of feeling real compassion for ourselves because we slow down and really see and feel our distress having an impact on us. Then our pain can awaken our desire and will to live in a new way. When we open to this awareness, it becomes unconditional presence, just being with what is, without any agenda.[6]

Some experiencers of spiritual awakening would like to hold on to the bliss and forget the rest. Kundalini energy doesn't work that way. It encompasses all of what we are as human beings, including our mental, emotional, physical and spiritual life. Holding on to the bliss of a Kundalini arousal and not processing the painful feelings is spiritual bypass, and a kind of high-level denial. It brings about a big imbalance and may be dangerous. The false self or shadow thereby becomes even stronger, exaggerating mental development as it controls the process, and in so doing, the ego becomes more inflated. In these extreme cases, what started out as personal transformation becomes a crisis and eventually, if the momentum continues, a psychotic break. If we feel our painful feelings, process them and let them go, our energy blocks are freed and we can experience endless energy. The more we are in touch with our Kundalini energy while remaining grounded, the easier time we will have being guided through our own process of wholeness and awakening.

## Projecting Feelings

As we grieve and see each painful memory dissolve, we may begin to realize that unconsciously we projected expected negativity onto others—a process called transference. Being able to see our own expectations and projections and how they work

---

[6] J.Welwood, "The Healing Power of Unconditional Presence."

to cloud our relationships and our reality is amazing.

Transference is like taking pictures with a camera that has a scratched and dirty lens. Every unhealed pain that we have buried inside is a smear on the lens of how we see our world. On our transformational journey we can buff and clean the lens by unlocking and releasing our painful memories a little at a time. As we do, we stop expecting others to treat us the way someone in our past did . . . and another scratch lifts from the lens. When we complete this work, we will be clear and can process our feelings as they happen, keeping the lens clean.

## Joyful Feelings

As we process old hurts and losses, we can begin to feel more alive and our hearts can stay open to feel joyful feelings. Remembering and releasing painful memories can free large amounts of energy for feeling and being alive. These feelings and emotions become fun as we experience the continuum toward unconditional love. The French *joie de vivre* means being alive is an extraordinary experience!

After a while this new appreciation for life hits us, and we realize that we do not have to stay in any one feeling. Feelings come and go, ebb and flow. We can experience them and then let them go. Experiencing our feelings shows we are alive and in touch with our world. Refusing to experience our feelings and burying them in our unconscious blocks our energy flow, and we keep scratching and smearing the lens of the way we see our life.

## Romantic Projection

Also called "irrational love projection," romantic projection is falling in love with someone who is completely inappropriate, or becoming completely enamored with a guru, teacher or therapist.[7] These projections can be common after

---

[7] Greenwell, *Energies of Transformation: A Guide to the Kundalini Process.*

Kundalini arousal, especially during a heart chakra opening. Kundalini symptoms and signs will be obvious during this period. Heart openings produce intense loving energy that is often projected onto someone and mistaken for romantic love, or as an overwhelming wave of compassion for the entire world. Healthy mystics channel this passion toward a love of God and of nature. The problem is overcome when we learn to stay grounded, stand firm at our center, maintain a healthy balance and love unconditionally.

The more I heal my relationships with my family of origin, the more "soul family" members I meet. A few of these relationships have a sacred bonding beyond this reality's understanding. Their essence is totally spiritual, with emotional and mental components. To reduce these relationships to the physical or romantic would be a disaster. As we continue in our transformational journey, more of these soul twins are likely to appear. While on a spiritual level this is a time of joy and celebration, it is also a time to use our positive ego or intellect and realize the implications of physically concertizing a relationship to be a lasting one. Are family units being broken up? Can you see the negatives or are you blinded at the moment?

Be careful after a heart chakra opening. Probably the best action is no action for a good while. During heart openings certain bonds can feel like great enchantment, but as the energy quiets down and life's obligations again sink in, this feeling of enchantment can transform into a curse. When a soul mate relationship becomes romantic involvement, all the ego-based emotions are reintroduced—jealousy, guilt, fear, shame, hurt, etc.

Unconditional love is not a familiar experience for most of us. Loving without a particular object to love is difficult to maintain. Projecting love before we are ready is dangerous. The romantic idea of soul mates or twin flames has seduced many during this vulnerable time, and then the rest of their life is based on this illusion of the beloved other, separate from the self. The beloved we seek elsewhere is really our own inner beloved. We can stop projecting the beloved outward and turn inward to fall madly in love in a healthy way, with ourselves and our lives.[8]

## Conclusion

After I came out of the body cast, occasionally I found myself in strange postures. When I was reading, a surge of energy might rush through me. I'd sit up and cross my legs, sometimes rocking for long periods of time. I'd continue to read, reasoning that I'd been in a body cast for so long that my body needed to do what it was doing. I tried to ignore it. Then I started experiencing, and occasionally still do, a warming in my chest. I feel my heart to be warmer than the rest of my body, a three-dimensional warm-to-hot feeling, exactly where my heart is. Kundalini rising to the heart chakra produces warm, intense, loving energy. This is an ecstatic and joyful feeling that can happen spontaneously after a spiritual awakening. At first it startled and scared me. Because we aren't prepared for all these wonderful new feelings, the period after a heart chakra opening may present some unusual problems.

My big breakthrough happened when I started volunteering in the emergency room of our local hospital and finally felt relief not only from the headaches I mentioned earlier, but also from the surges of energy and the strange sensations in my heart. When I placed my hands on critically ill patients, I could feel the energy drain through my arms and out my palms. I could see the patient's coloring get better, and many times they would tell me that their pain medication was finally working. I experienced the uncomfortable surges of energy in my body *transforming* into endless enthusiasm for my

---

[8] Greyson and Harris, 1989; Small, 1991.

new work. The love and warmth in my heart connected to a burning sensation in the palm of my hands, which was my sign to touch someone who needed it.

The sense of emptiness I had lived with most of my life had been filled in my NDE as I reconnected with my Source. Now, just a few years later, I could feel it every time I placed my hands on a patient. When I helped someone in this manner, I felt the connection to God and to my patient. I was filled by my relationship to both. As I help others in this way, I become stronger. So service is the vehicle that connects me to God, myself and others. Going back to school and becoming a respiratory and massage therapist has given me access to this kind of service every day. Working with this energy has made it apparent and almost concrete to me. And this work has given me a creative outlet for all this love that I have felt since my spiritual awakening. This outlet is the answer for the dilemma of a heart opening. The unconditional love of a heart opening, so unfamiliar to most of us, does not need and cannot be restricted to a particular love object. In essence, we are falling in love with the Universe and our own core. After a heart opening, it can be difficult to distinguish the two.[9]

Before meeting Ken Ring and Bruce Greyson and finding the literature on Kundalini, I was constantly puzzled when I allowed my critical rational side to try to figure out what was happening. Visualizing light and colors in a dark room was impossible to explain, so I avoided thinking about it. Soon, the coincidences and synchronicities became so playful in my mind that I accepted them as my own little secret with the Universe. However, keeping all this in balance forced me into hours alone so I could contemplate and, without understanding what I was doing, meditate and pray. But I didn't think of it as prayer because it wasn't memorized from any writings. It felt like I was attempting to talk to God. In meditation, I was listening. In my own natural way, everything I

---

[9] Greyson and Harris, 1989.

was doing was supporting and encouraging this energy to continue to burn away blocks and move up through my body, connecting me more completely to my soul/spirit.

I returned to psychotherapy when I felt I needed it. Whatever I have needed along this path has appeared for me at the right time, as if being swept into a beautiful current. Since my NDE, I have read constantly, usually three, four or five books at a time. No fiction. I am always hungry for information, knowledge and wisdom. Once I understood more about all this, my mantra during uncomfortable Kundalini symptoms was, "This is natural. This is all right! This is evolution!" I could almost visualize my nervous system going into overdrive, as Ring wrote in *Heading Toward Omega.*

I have heard hundreds of stories of energy awakenings and collectively with Ken and Bruce, over a thousand stories of spiritual experiences and then manifestations of the energy. We agree that most people who experience Kundalini energy have not had a full awakening. Instead, the energy may rise only to a certain level, opening chakras and freeing blocks, then sink back into dormancy and inactivity. This new consciousness/energy can be interpreted on the emotional or feeling level as unconditional love. Eventually, that conscious energy will turn inward to free us of our old neurotic tapes and heal us physically, mentally, emotionally and spiritually. The idea is not to stop it, but to give it every opportunity to work and grow while maintaining our center by staying grounded in a balanced lifestyle.

This has become my life's work, both personally and professionally. I have perceived these Kundalini awakenings as an opening, not an accomplishment in myself or others I have met and sometimes treated. This mechanism is built into each human naturally and is part of every one of us. It balances the development of body, spirit and mind, which deepens our understanding and appreciation of the wonders of existence, and leads the psyche toward peaceful coexistence with the

natural cycles of living and dying. It is a natural cycle, a natural response to becoming a more whole and spiritual person—which puts us into harmony with our deepest potential,
with the larger community of our beloved planet Earth, and
with God, our infinite source of unconditional love.

# SEVEN

# Mind Split or Whole in the Head?

The human brain is divided into two separate hemi-spheres, the left and the right, and joined in the center by a large nerve track called the corpus callosum. Both sides of the brain have different but complementary functions. They process information differently and in varying levels of intensity. Each side thinks in its own way. *Each side also speaks to us differently.*

Until recently, the right hemisphere was thought of as the minor of the two, while the left was major in our functioning. But our judgment was detrimental because the right hemisphere is the gateway to the spiritual and the transcendental. There has been a lot written recently about left and right brain research. I started reading about it after my NDE because I needed answers to explain why my perceptions and learning abilities had changed so dramatically. I have heard from most experiencers that they have had a shift in brain functioning after a spiritual awakening. Because this is a complex subject, in this chapter I will continue to describe some of these concepts as part of my personal story for easier understanding.

## My Splitting Head!

When my body cast came off I swore that I would always be well and never need medical help or tests again. Then I experienced four migraine headaches within a period of two months. Sitting in a lab waiting to have an electroencephalogram, I ate my sworn words. The test was normal. The headaches lost their intensity after awhile when I learned to meditate and give myself lots of alone time. Looking back on it now, I realize that my "splitting" headaches came from the two sides of my brain disagreeing, and my left logical side trying to censor the new feelings and creativity of my right hemisphere. I still get a headache occasionally, usually when I have been overwhelmed emotionally and haven't had a chance to process what I am feeling.

I realized that my brain was functioning differently, since my time perception had somehow changed or slowed down. Something weird was going on. Time didn't feel linear anymore. It seemed to exist in cycles. Cycles inside of cycles. Days felt different. The weeks cycled. My moods had cycles. I recognized that my husband and children had their own cyclic rhythm, too. Sometimes we would be in the same cyclic space at the same moment, and even little things became spectacular.

Early one evening, five months after my cast came off, my five-year-old son, Gary, came running into the house, all muddy, screaming about the fish he had just seen in the creek. Within minutes he and I were leaning over the bank of the creek with my kitchen strainer, catching a few "fish" to get a better look. We must have carried back 30 tadpoles in a big bucket. He and I were on the front porch on our knees, staring into the bucket, mesmerized. I could see that this fascination shared with one of my children connected us powerfully into the moment. Gary and I were together just as though we were in a bubble, the kind I described in my life review.

From catching tadpoles all the way to the greatest of life's moments, the quality or the texture of the experience has to do with our mind and which side of the brain we are using. We call these experiences bubbles, in part, because we have just had a direct experience of the moment mediated through our brain's right hemisphere. When our minds function this way, the left doesn't divide us from the experience by analyzing or intellectualizing. If we keep our minds functioning like a camera, just keep taking pictures, we can see or perceive through our right hemisphere. This is also called seeing with our hearts.

Many experiencers agree with the bubble metaphor. They tell of spontaneous experiences sprinkled through their lives after their initial awakening that are similar in texture to the original one where again they can "see." They use terms like "grace" and "spirit." They feel/see great meaning and express a sense of timelessness.

## Peak Experience

Abraham Maslow was one of the foremost spokesmen of humanistic psychology, also called the Third Force. He studied many of these experiences. He probably would call my tadpole experience a plateau experience. The major experiences, NDEs and all kinds of spiritual awakenings, he called peak experiences. It is easy to understand his pioneering spirit in transpersonal psychology after reading about his own awakening:

> My experience of being bored in an academic procession and feeling slightly ridiculous in cap and gown,

and suddenly slipping over into being a symbol under the aspect of eternity rather than just a bored and irritated individual in the moment and in the specific place. My vision or imagining was that the academic procession stretched way, way out into the future, far, far away, further than I could see, and it had Socrates at its head, and the implication was, I suppose, that many of the people far ahead had been there and in previous generations, and that I was a successor and a follower of all the great academics and professors and intellectuals. Then the vision was also of the procession stretching out behind me into a dim, hazy infinity where there were people not yet born who would join the academic procession, the procession of scholars, of intellectuals, of scientists and philosophers. And I thrilled at being in such a procession and felt the great dignity of it, of my robes, and even of myself as a person who belonged in this procession. That is, I became a symbol; I stood for something outside my own skin. I was not exactly an individual. I was also a "role" of the eternal teacher. I was the Platonic essence of the teacher.[1]

Many people report having peak experiences after their initial spiritual awakening. After a period of learning, growing into wholeness, they level off to having extensive plateau experiences. They tell us that every day contains the consciousness they enjoyed during their initial experience. They are mediating reality through the right side of their brain.

## Traits of Each Hemisphere

The soft gentle voice of intuition is activated through the right hemisphere of our brain. Our logical left hemisphere doesn't want to believe in intuition or something as unusual as Kundalini, or for that matter, near-death experiences, spiritual awakenings, cyclic time or creativity. These come from the right hemisphere, and the left feels threatened, wanting

---

[1] Maslow, *The Farther Reaches of Human Nature.*

to remain in control. There is nothing logical about seeing God in birds and trees. In fact, there's nothing logical at all about the right hemisphere. Logic belongs to the left hemisphere. If we've spent our lives in a rational logical left hemisphere world, as most of us in the West have, we can't understand words like consciousness, perception, intuition, revelation and mystical.

The chart on the following page shows some important functions of the two hemispheres of our brain. It's easy to see how they are different, even opposing, although they are complementary.

We in the West have been taught to suppress our right hemisphere traits, cutting ourselves off from half of who we are. Our left hemisphere once dictated our beliefs that now seem obsolete as we move further in our journey toward wholeness. When we awaken spiritually, we open to both sides of our brain. If you *want* to awaken spiritually, start by honoring these right hemisphere functions in your own inner life and the outer world. Our right hemisphere can delight us with new ways to absorb knowledge and intuit reality. It helps us to remember all of who we really are. Our right hemisphere in balance with our left functions on levels we never could have imagined were possible, giving us the tools to grow and truly create ourselves.

## Traits of Each Hemisphere of the Brain
(taken in part from C.L. Whitfield, *Spirituality in Recovery*.)

| Left Hemisphere | Right Hemisphere |
| --- | --- |
| Mind | Self |
| Rational, linear | Intuitive, creative |
| Verbal | Quiet |
| Understandable | Paradoxical |
| Obvious | Subtle |
| Knowledge | Wisdom |
| Doing | Non-doing |
| Controlling | Letting go |
| Fear | Love |
| Chaos | Peace |
| Causal | Acausal |
| Hard | Soft |
| Form | Formless |
| Microcosm | Macrocosm |
| Closed | Open |
| Many | One |
| Psychoanalytic | Transpersonal |
| Behavioral | Humanistic |
| Yang | Yin |
| Time | Space |
| Day | Night |
| Head | Heart |
| Content | Process |
| Thinking | Feeling |
| Sensation | Intuition |
| Persona | Shadow |
| Outlook | Insight |
| Outer focus | Inner focus |
| Ego | Being |
| Science—old paradigm | Science—new paradigm |
| Scientist | Mystic |
| Religion (conventional) | Spirituality |
| Skepticism | Faith |
| Reason | Imagination |
| Objective | Subjective |
| Finite | Infinite |
| Active | Contemplative |
| Autonomy | Dependence |
| Cognition | Perception |
| Rote prayer | Spontaneous prayer |

# Psychic Abilities and Healthy Boundaries

As a by-product of spiritual awakening and the transformational journey, a variety of psychic abilities or higher sense perceptions usually manifest.[1] They will also begin to emerge in our awareness without having a dramatic spiritual awakening first, simply by developing our right hemisphere traits. This is nothing new. Psychic abilities have been a general assumption of the world's traditional spiritual teachings over the millennia. This is consistent with Ring's and my view that the NDE serves principally as a catalyst for spiritual awakening and development and that psychic abilities usually manifest as a by-product. This interpretation is also supported by the work of other independent researchers.

---

[1] I first learned this term in a book that has become a classic, called *Breakthrough to Creativity—Your Higher Sense Perception,* by Shafica Karagulla, M.D.

Ring says that the ancient literature of the great spiritual psychologies links psychic phenomena to the unfolding of higher consciousness. But there is usually a warning included about the dangers of becoming attached to the psychic phenomena. From the Buddhist perspective, the attainment of such powers is only a minor advantage, and it is of no value in itself for progress toward liberation. In one who has not yet attained the state of Nirvana, these psychic abilities are seen as an impediment, and may endanger progress by enhancing and strengthening our attachment to our false self.[2] We can, however, celebrate these higher sense perceptions because they serve as a reminder that we are connected, that our subtle energy fields overlap and act upon one another, sometimes even at great distances.

## Pitfalls

As the masters of the ancient spiritual psychologies warned, focusing on the talent of psychic ability will create attachments that distract us. Many people get caught in this trap. It seems to be so provocative that it becomes a kind of stopping off point. Then after a while, the person tends to incorporate it into normal reality. As our transformational journey continues, we realize that these higher sense perceptions are wonderful when used with humility and in the act of service.

Psychic abilities are our birthright as human beings. However, if a sudden spiritual experience causes them to emerge quickly instead of gradually, it can overpower us because it disrupts our boundaries. For that reason, we can acknowledge and respect psychic abilities as being a possible pitfall. In the Omega Project, experiencers reported becoming more moody. With a sudden increase in psychic sensitivity, we're going to pick up others moods and feelings more than we did before starting on our spiritual path.

---

[2] Ring 1984, quote from Golman.

Another possible pitfall is trying to hurry psychic develop-ment by taking lessons or classes from a teacher about whom we know little. Before doing so, read books by authors who are respected in the field and who show humility and integri-ty in their life's work and private life. To become more aware of psychic abilities, it is also helpful to learn meditation. Through meditation we become fine-tuned to the subtle lev-els of our inner life. When we then know our inner life well, by focusing and centering we can go behind it or quiet it down and sense these psychic perceptions.

Community classes on psychic abilities need to be screened carefully, and even then, use your gut feelings. If you feel uncomfortable or even faintly afraid, then something is probably not right with what you have chosen. Psychic teachers can carry contagious emotional and psychological pathology. Any emotional or mental pathology they are car-rying, even unconscious material, can be projected onto you through your perhaps vulnerable boundaries.

Some people explore psychic realms for ego enhancement rather than for spirituality and self-transformation. Psychic gifts can be big temptations for power seekers. As happened in "The Sorcerer's Apprentice" in Disney's animated *Fantasia*, these power junkies may soon learn in dramatic ways the limits of their power. This is something to be aware of, and if you feel it happening to you, you can work through this stage by surrounding yourself with self-actualized people who show humility and integrity.

Bruce Greyson and I got panicky phone calls occasion-ally from experiencers who had waking visions or dreams predicting great catastrophe, such as fires or the end of the world. There are many ways to look at these. The inter-pretation I like to use is Jungian: these waking visions or dreams are our unconscious talking to us in symbols and may reflect what is or could happen in our own inner life. This is also the way the people I like to be around own and keep a well-balanced attitude toward their higher sense perceptions.

Of course, there is always the exception to the rule. We had phone calls about the Challenger blowing up days before it happened. Callers were greatly agitated and I understand why. The problem for people who get attached to visions of catastrophes is that they feel responsible and driven to warn and stop the disaster, but they can't identify the plane or the place. When the next air disaster happens, they are sure that they predicted it. Then they suffer from great guilt, as though they had been a contributing cause, and beneath the guilt, perhaps, denial of ego inflation. I have counseled clients with this dilemma and there is no easy solution. These people have to work hard at staying balanced about their guilt and not focus their identity only on this ability because this way of thinking can and will eventually create disaster for their own psyche.

In 1986 I spoke at a conference sponsored by West Georgia State College's Psychology Department on "Clinical Parapsychology." We dialogued on problems like the above. Now they offer several classes for counseling approaches to patients who have a variety of psychic abilities mixed in with mental and emotional problems. These troubled people are unable to differentiate between what is psychic and what is pathological. They have no definition of where they end and others begin, and where reality begins and ends. They lack healthy boundaries. It is good to see these problems finally being addressed on a college level to at least a few students of psychology.

## Learning Experiences

If you want to take a class in any of these areas, find out what is being offered at your local community college or public school's adult education evening program. Check with others who have already taken the class.

The most rewarding classes I have taken have been on healing techniques from nurses or well-known healers such as Delores Krieger, Ph.D., and Dora Kunz. They developed "Therapeutic Touch," a master's degree program for nurses at New York University. Ten years ago, at the first of two of their workshops that I've taken, Dr. Krieger taught us how to center. She said that 4,000 nurses had already taken her course and all but a few could do it.

## Bioenergy Balancing

Bioenergy balancing was the most generic term I could think of when I opened my own breath and body work practice. I don't consider myself a student of any one technique. Also, I don't identify any group or culture as having a monopoly on the energy used in healing. I do know that there is living energy coming through and balancing the energy of the client. Therefore, I call what I do "bioenergy balancing."

In a session I visualize a Light source coming from the Universe that is carrying healing energy. I do not do the balancing; it is done through me. I do not have a planned outcome, nor am I attached to any particular outcome. I center, clearing my outer mind of mental activity. I have a clear intent to help. Then I pray, inviting the healing energy into my self, picturing my self as a hollow tube with hands on the client where the current will flow. I become aware of warmth or an actual sense of a current flowing out through the palms of my hands. I trust the wisdom of the Higher Process and continue where my hands and my heart take me. Once I am aware of the current, which can take anywhere from two to 15 minutes, I feel like a child at play. I'm not using my intellect to plan what to do next. I'm moved by the energy, just playing with it.

I can use a light-touch Shiatsu or polarity method, just accessing the energy. I stay aware of my client's breathing patterns, and when necessary I coach the client to keep the breath steady and deep. I also use massage techniques that work deeply into the muscle, such as cross-fiber massage or trigger point work.[3] Most of the time my clients go into an altered state of consciousness, occasionally seeing colors or scenes, or they just enjoy a floating sensation. They usually stay on the table for 10 to 30 minutes afterwards.

During the entire session I rely on a state of consciousness beyond this one, more than I do on any one technique. I was assisting people by doing hands-on work before I became a massage therapist. The deep massage I do now is for releasing stress and realigning muscle structure. This type of deep work is more effective with deep, slow, breath work. The client is coached actually to blow the stress out with the release of the muscle.

While I always include bioenergy balancing or healing work with massage, I don't always use massage when assisting people in their healing. An example would be clients with cancer who need physical touch because they have walled themselves off from their bodies, which contain the enemy. This tightens them to the point where they can actually constrict the flow of medication. I use light touch, and sometimes I don't even move my hands around at all. I place my right hand just below their navel and my left over their heart or forehead, say my prayer, center and stay like that for 15 or 20 minutes. This gentle method entrains them into the same state of consciousness that I am in.

Sometimes I will start this type of session by telling them to visualize each part of their body relaxing, and I will coach them to relaxing breath patterns. The reason I don't use massage with cancer clients is that massage creates better lymph drainage, which could spread the cancer if the cells are already in the lymph system. This method is soothing and stress-removing and helps lessen pain, with or without pain

---

[3] Travell, *Myofascial Pain and Dysfunction.*

medication. It's especially advisable for use every evening after chemotherapy and can be taught to safe family and friends of the client. Or I will organize a healing team of volunteers to take turns. This is safe and a gift of compassion at the same time.

## Centering

Centering is a focusing within. I ask for God's help and visualize a pillar of white light coming down and into the top of my head and flowing out through my heart and hands. This is from where compassion radiates, and at that point I feel it for my client. My intention then is to extend love and to help the client by relaxing my conscious mind and observing the Universal energies flowing through me and then into the client. This healing energy has its own wisdom to help balance and make whole. I believe that this centering and extending process is the key to using any type of psychic ability. We relax and center, turning off the part of our minds that communicates in words so that a deeper, more primal and basic sense can be observed.

This centering process is a function of the right hemisphere of the brain. After a spiritual awakening our right hemisphere traits tend to become more active, and centering and meditation will usually come more easily. Here we are non-logical, non-linear and beyond normal time. Through meditation or another process of quieting ourself, we can still our language-dominated left hemisphere. The problem here is that the more I describe this process to you with words, the farther away we may get from the experience of centering.

Centering involves no words. When my left hemisphere tries to get in and judge or chatter, I picture myself as a camera in the act of recording the scene by seeing and feeling my inner life. Then I can recognize any psychic information surfacing from my inner life. What I am centering into is my actual experience of my True Self. While assisting another in a hands-on healing, after 15 or 20 minutes my left brain chatter will start again and behind it I will have an urge to say thank you to the Universe.[4] In the spirit of compassion, healing evokes a sense of humility. After a healing, I say a silent prayer of thanks and leave the room. Finally, I shake my hands and run cold water over them to break the connection and re-activate my own healthy boundaries.

## What Is Psychic?

A person who can perceive multidimensional aspects of reality is psychic. In our ordinary state of consciousness our minds take in vast amounts of data. Our brains are in constant motion, negotiating our focus and screening out the excess. While doing so is essential for conducting our normal affairs, it can upstage our True Self, which is already and inherently psychic.[5] The True Self has access to a wider range of incoming information, some of which is subtle. The ability to sense in these deeper ways through centering in the True Self is natural. This knowledge can communicate through symbols, as in dreams or waking visions, flashes of a scene that are so fast that they register as a sudden memory more than a vision, and in numerous other ways.

This knowledge also communicates through a direct, intuitive knowing. I may sometimes perceive it through a felt sense, and sometimes it is just there within me. When I am in this state, my information does not come from feeling the other person. I recognize this information within me, within my own inner life, and I can recognize it as not my own. Occasionally, *deja vu* comes into what would otherwise be an ordinary scene. I feel like I have done this before. What I call "future memories" register in the same way deja vu does, but I have a felt sense that this is part of the future.

---

[4] I prefer to call this activity helping, because my role is as a helper. The actual healing is co-created between the client and God.
[5] True Self may also be called Core Self, Child Within, soul, heart and so on.

I can sometimes even see this multidimensional reality. There are fields—emotional, mental, spiritual—surrounding physical form. As in an aura, these fields are made of radiant energies that have varying degrees of color and surround us like a giant, semi-transparent egg. Our fields may interact with other people's fields, giving us information about the other. There are many people today operating in high positions that have these abilities, and this is one reason why they are successful. Whether in politics, education, corporations, science or the creative arts, what we have called creativity and genius come in part from these abilities. Very few if any of these gifted people talk about their higher abilities. They just do their work and they usually do it well.

## Psychic Abilities and Relationships

We may first become aware of this multidimensional reality or felt sense in a close loving relationship. When I teach, students tell me of having this special connection with their boyfriend or girlfriend, at times knowing the phone is going to ring, knowing when the other is unhappy or hurt. They tell me that what the other person feels, they too feel, whether it is joyful or painful. I suggest that they stay with the subtlety of the feeling. We can do so by tuning out the outer mind and focusing on the vague feeling of direct or intuitive knowing, the process of centering. We can have direct access to our subconscious mind and even beyond to the transpersonal or super-conscious mind. By being open to our inner life and ignoring the usual noise and preconceived ideas of the outer world, we are free to explore the multilevel aspects of our reality. This is a kind of fine-tuning of our inner life that can allow us to perceive these fields.

In *Full Circle,* I told the story of my experience of picking up my mother's feelings 1,700 miles away, when she was in a hospital. I felt a pain in my upper leg at the same time she was having a bone marrow biopsy on her upper leg. My leg gave way from the shock of the pain and I fell. I had no knowledge beforehand of her having a painful procedure. When I talked with her on the phone the next day and she told me, I realized that her biopsy happened at the same moment as my fall. Psychic connectedness to the people we love transcends the boundaries of space and time, since they don't follow the same laws. It can be useful to be aware of these kinds of experiences and of your increasing abilities. Some of the pain, moodiness or misery that you are picking up is not your own, and you can learn how to protect yourself through strengthening your boundaries.

When I began having these kinds of experiences, I wanted more. After a while, though, I realized that what I really wanted was definition, usefulness and protection. I now often picture or see another person's egg-shaped pattern of energy or aura as they approach me. As we talk, I am aware that their egg is overlapping and sometimes encompassing my egg. If I don't like what I feel, I will step back a few feet. Sometimes I'll even put up my hands at about heart level, holding them tactfully away as if playing with the tips of my fingers. When we walk away in separate directions, in my mind's eye I picture them taking all of their stuff from their egg back with them. I might even do a psychic housecleaning by visualizing my own egg filled with white Light, and perhaps even visualize their egg filled with white Light, too.

## Telepathic Knowing

Telepathy is so much a part of my everyday life that I never think of myself as being telepathic. I perceive the world as having that telepathic level where we are all connected. Often, just minutes or seconds before my daughter, Beth, calls me long distance, I will think of her. When I call any of my children they will often tell me they were just thinking of me. We love each other and are connected, even though we live hundreds of miles apart.

Sometimes a song is playing in my mind, and when I will turn on the radio, the song is playing. Or I will delay leaving the house, and then a package arrives that the delivery person could not have left without my signature. It feels good to be aware of these little telepathic knowings. It gives me a sense that the world is put together better than the evening news leads us to believe.

We are conditioned early in life to communicate with words. Then our thoughts appear in sequential patterns in our minds and in our speech. A primary sense, telepathy, happens before words and sequential thoughts. While doing bioenergy balancing in my work as a massage and respiratory therapist, I can pick up a feeling that a client is still unaware of and ask if the client might be feeling it right now. My information of a feeling is coming from my own inner life, but I can recognize it as not being my own. If I am trying to figure out in words what my client's feeling is, then that is not telepathy.

A few times I have been naive enough to use my psychic abilities with my family, and it has backfired. I found out quickly that I was invading their boundaries, their privacy. I then realized that my false self, or ego, can't always be out of the way when I am so personally involved. Occasionally now, someone close to me will ask for my help. I am careful to stay objective, keeping my own agenda out, or I just say I can't do it. Then I offer them the opportunity to hear my opinion. The water gets murky when working on a psychic level with family members. I don't recommend it, and I try to be respectful of others' boundaries and not jump in. This is a hard lesson and requires psychic maturity, trusting and knowing intuitively when to speak and when to be silent.

## Public Speaking

Higher sense perceptions are often remarkable for me when I speak to a group. If I focus on the audience's auras,

I see them going from individual auras to one huge egg-shaped aura, encompassing everyone. As the mood changes during a story that I am telling, the group aura changes. When I am finished and everyone claps, the aura breaks back down to individual auras. Clapping may serve more purposes than we think. I also have a felt sense of my audience, and that intuitively guides me in the direction of my topics and my intensity. And naturally, it helps during the question and answer period.

I believe that telepathy and other psychic abilities are natural and that we no longer need to separate them as being unusual, paranormal or supernatural. They are part of our everyday experience. We can thus be more aware of our perceptions, just as we can become more aware of reality being limited only by our beliefs. The less we limit ourselves through rigid beliefs, the bigger our reality gets. I have asked several other public speakers, and they say that their intuition and higher sense perceptions also guide them in some of the ways I have just described. At this level we experience the feeling of being unified within our self and our audience.

## Psychic and Spiritual Healing

When observing auras before I assist patients in their healing process, small waves or kinks in their auras indicate a problem. I can also discern problems by comparing the density that I see throughout the auras. This ability first appeared when I saw a murky or foggy look around others' physical body. If the fog was translucent and evenly consistent overall, the people usually reported feeling balanced and healthy. If I saw murky disturbances and eventually kinks, it usually indicated that they were having some kind of pain or distress. These disturbances can be smoothed out with a wave of the hand through the area, or by placing my hands in direct contact and holding it for

10 or 15 minutes. An introductory book that explains how to do this is *Your Healing Hands*.[6]

My intuition tells me, and I then ask if they feel that they might benefit from, or are armored against, a series of healing treatments, usually three to five over as many days. If they have children or a safe family member or other close person at home, the best arrangement would be for me to show them how to do what I had done and turn it over to the safe person. Or I make arrangements to do it myself and/or organize a volunteer group to take turns visiting and providing this healing assistance to the person who needs it. As I said earlier, this can also work well with cancer patients who are receiving chemotherapy.

One of my most rewarding memories about working with dying patients comes from when we invited the grandchildren, ages two and older, to do a group healing on the grandparent. Kids naturally know what is going on and welcome the opportunity.[7]

You don't have to be clairvoyant to be able to help someone. Being able to see the fields or auras is not necessary. What is necessary is a sincere desire to help the other person. Spiritual healing or helping can be transmitted by intent from the healer to the one healed. Many times I have watched hospice nurses put their arm around a patient's shoulder and establish eye contact; then the patient and nurse would smile at each other. The patient's aura brightened immediately, and the patient usually felt better for hours.

In medicine's old paradigm, it was believed that the death of a patient meant failure. That created a negative attitude around a dying patient and isolated them. The new paradigm recognizes the fact that sometimes our patients die and that compassion plus safe physical touch is what may help them

[6] Gordon, *Your Healing Hands*, 1979.
[7] Ibid.

the most. I have seen dying patients contracted in pain, even though they are being given large amounts of narcotics. When a nurse or when I gently put our hands on them, they tend to relax, their physical positioning opens up, their coloring gets better and they will announce a little while later that they are free of pain. This is by no means a medical failure. Everyone is going to die someday. If we can help with the quality of life until then through compassion and touch, I call that a success.

## Boundaries

When I am in session with a client, I often feel awareness of heat, pain or pressure in the same area the client is feeling pain, although not at the same intensity. I have developed a sensitivity to what other people are feeling. This sensitivity is close *empathy*, understanding what the other person is feeling without identifying personally. It is observation and a kind of understanding without taking on another's pain. This is a complex area. I am feeling what my client feels, but I do not identify with it as my own. To make sure that I don't identify, as I discussed earlier, I have a ritual of shaking my hands and washing them in cold water to break the connection and reactivate my own healthy boundaries. "Boundaries" means distinguishing and keeping out what is not me, and holding in place what is.

Before I had my NDE, I was a sponge for others' emotional pain, because I had never developed healthy boundaries. In my life review I saw myself as a child enmeshed in my mother's pain, both her physical pain and her mental/emotional problems. As an adult, still enmeshed, I could feel other people's pain and thought it was my own. I walled myself off from my mother by putting long-distance physical boundaries between us. For months at a time I would find excuses not to be with her, or I would move to the other side of town and eventually out of state. However, distance alone could not heal my woundedness. *I needed to develop healthy boundaries,* and at the same time realize that we are all connected.[8]

Learning about psychic abilities, rituals such as shaking and washing my hands, and using white Light in my aura have given me ways to create healthy boundaries. An even more important way that I have helped myself is to go back developmentally and give myself a second chance to develop my boundaries both in therapy and workshops, and in reading the literature on healthy boundaries.[9]

After our spiritual awakenings, for those of us who desire to help others, we need to help and heal ourselves first. Many of us are wounded healers. We may help others, but we may also continue being victims of our own wounds. Functioning in any capacity with any of these higher sense perceptions, we will pick up and possibly not be able to throw off others' problems. We need to define and heal our own boundary distortions before we can function in healthy relationships and as healthy helping professionals.

Eventually we may know when the time is appropriate to focus on our higher sense perceptions. We can open in deep trust to the process because we will trust our own judgment. While these psychic signals are in our awareness most of the time, we have the choice to act on and use them, or ignore them and also the confidence in our own sorting abilities to recognize what is mine and what isn't. If I decide that it is appropriate to act, I then answer in honesty, all the while being in a boundless state of consciousness. I set aside my sense of separateness, my boundaries, and join for a time with the other.

This kind of psychic rapport cannot flourish when people conceive of themselves as isolated in thought and feeling.

---

[8] See *Boundaries and Relationships*, by Charles Whitfield, 1993.
[9] Whitfield, 1993.

This kind of boundlessness leads to a freedom and openness that is rare in most forms of human communication. But remember, no matter how developed our psychic ability is, we can get hurt without healthy boundaries to define me from not-me.

## Learning to Set Healthy Boundaries

About boundaries, Charles Whitfield says, "A boundary or limit is how far we can comfortably go in a relationship and how far someone else can comfortably go with us. A boundary is not just a mental construct: Our boundaries are real. Other people's boundaries are real."

Boundaries and limits serve a useful purpose: they protect the well-being and integrity of our True Self, our Child Within. Our awareness of boundaries and limits first helps us discover who we are. Until we know who we are, it will be difficult for us to have healthy relationships of any sort. Without an awareness of boundaries, it is difficult to sort out who is unsafe to be around, including people who are toxic for us and people who may mistreat or abuse us.

Once we have a spiritual awakening, our unconscious material from our inner life comes into our conscious awareness in powerful ways. It becomes increasingly easier to see what is ours as opposed to what we are picking up from others. We can now actually recognize when we are stuffing—repressing or suppressing—our own hurts or traumas. With this new awareness comes new choices. We can identify ourselves as awakening spiritual human beings. We can experience this material from our unconscious for our own personal growth and well-being. And we can ask God to help us co-create better ways.

Being aware of and expressing parts of our inner life without blaming others require a delicate balance. We can learn to hear the shared inner life of others without taking on what is not ours. Distinguishing and keeping out what is not-me and holding in place what is me takes time, patience and practice. Healthy boundaries help us in this balance.[10]

I have been a student of my own inner life for almost 20 years. I had no choice. I was suddenly awakened, not only to my spiritual connection, but to the emotional connection of my True Self, and it was letting me know it needed protection. After years of studying and experiencing personal growth, it is becoming more fun to observe all of this going on in my inner life. I watch my psychic ability coming from my True Self. I trust my inner life negotiating when to stay open and when to activate my boundaries. I see my *positive* ego stepping in to protect my innocent child/True Self. I can still hear my *negative* ego/false self doing a good imitation of dedication and loving friendship as it tries to take back control. My inner life is pretty busy. I have to stay on my toes and stay aware of who's running the show. And then in meditation and during play or any conscious centering; I can relax, letting everyone inside quiet down and allow the Light of unconditional love to wash through.

## Psychic Abilities and Healthy Boundaries: A Story

Several years ago I was asked to travel to another state to talk to a support group for bereaved parents. I had talked to support groups for bereaved parents before and said I would go gladly.

The calls over the next several weeks, however, were distressing. This particular group was split. Half wanted me to come and half said no, which was surprising. I finally agreed to come on a Sunday instead of their usual meeting time during the week. One couple had offered to have the meeting in their home instead of the usual community meeting hall, and because of the disagreement this was not an official meeting.

---

[10] Harris, 1990; Whitfield, 1991, 1993.

With that little information, I agreed to do a one-and-a-half-hour talk. As long as I would be back home by sunset, I would trust the Universe and whatever it had in store for me.

I found myself praying long and hard during the three-hour drive. I was met at a designated point by a pleasant couple who drove the rest of the way and told me the details of their child's death as we pulled up to a lovely suburban home. Walking inside was like walking through a wall. There were palpable layers of hostility acting like a fog that filled the large living room. (This is the multidimensional reality I have been referring to.) The expressions on the faces of the 20 to 30 people confirmed what my sensitivity told me.

I talked for about 45 minutes, telling my NDE story and summing up what we now know from the research, and then asked for questions. Their response was full of anger and much of that anger was aimed at me. Who did I think I was, coming to adjust them? I continued to hear their questions and building rage. My observer self was praying, hoping for a lead into some kind of resolution to whatever was going on. I was not taking any of the attack personally. I was clear on the fact when I accepted this particular talk that I hadn't done anything to trigger the original debate and wasn't doing anything now to provoke the kind of hostility I was hearing. I could almost see them projecting their anger at me. This perception helped me to continue feeling centered within my self and deflect what they were throwing at me.

I told them several times that there was no way I could begin to understand their pain. All I could do was share with them my experience of what it felt like to die. Part of me decided it was time to get out as soon as the opportunity appeared. This group was too tough and I was not skilled enough. This was a job for someone more experienced. I was drained. I had nothing more to offer them.

From the beginning I had no intention of fixing them. I had wanted to help, but I certainly didn't need to feel that I had helped. I just wanted to go home. I had promised myself from the beginning that I would be in my car by three o'clock and home before sunset. But before I left, out of curiosity or whatever, I said, "You all seem so angry. Some of you lost your child 20 years ago and some of you, only a month or two. Just tell me, if you gave up your anger, if you just let it go, what would be so wrong? Would or could you still be connected to your dead child without anger? Is it the anger that keeps you connected? Why can't you give up the anger and be connected with love?"

One man was so upset that he got up and left the house, slamming the door behind him. Others started answering me, but the emotion that was pouring out reached an even higher level of intensity than before. Everyone was claiming more pain than anyone else. The argument elevated to who was suffering more, the men or the women. I hadn't been able to connect a man and a woman as a couple this whole time. And now this meeting turned into the men against the women. Instead of picking up connections linking couples as I usually can, what became apparent was the immense walls, the armoring that divided the two camps. These people had built walls with their grief, and their egos were defending their walls. They were all in their heads, defending against moving into their hearts.

Just when I thought that I couldn't take any more, the hostess announced that we were taking a coffee and donut break. Thankfully, I got up from my chair to move toward the kitchen, noticing the glances I was getting from the others already standing around the table. None of the glances looked friendly. Standing next to me was a short balding man with a mustache. "I have a headache. I think I'll have to go home," he said weakly to me.

"Wait," I said. "Let me help you." I really felt that way. I never offer to put my hands on someone if I don't have an active feeling of wanting to help. This man must have caught my compassion immediately and agreed. "I'll put my hands on your head for a few minutes. It doesn't hurt and it may take away your headache."

We walked into another room. I took off my rings and watch. He sat on a straight-back chair, and I placed my right hand on the back of his neck with my palm in direct contact with his spine and the outside of my index finger running along the bottom edge of his skull. The palm of my left hand was in direct contact with the center of his forehead. I centered my self and said my usual prayer. The next 10 or 15 minutes flew by. I said a prayer of thanks and went into the other room to wash my hands in cold water. And then I went back to check on him. He looked at me with a kind but shy look and said, "I can't believe it. My headache's gone."

When we walked back into the living room his shyness quickly turned into a proclamation—"My headache's gone. I had a headache and she took it away."

"Oh, great!" I thought. "Now they're going to burn me at the stake." Everyone was talking at the same time. Questions were being thrown at me about how I did it. And then it hit me. Of course, why not? We had done enough talking. In fact, we had done perhaps too much talking. These people needed compassion, not only for themselves, but for each other.

"Okay!" I announced. "The first part of the day is over. For those of you who want to stay a couple more hours, we are going to learn how to remove headaches. We are going to do hands-on healings. Husbands and wives form teams. One of you sits while the other stands to the left of the person sitting." My one-and-a-half-hour talk went four and a half hours more than I had originally planned. I was there a total of seven hours. I was taken to dinner. I got home at one o'clock in the morning.

What happened over the next four and a half hours was really touching, no pun intended. No more finger-pointing and raging. No more announcements that one spouse was suffering more than the other. Couples touched each other all afternoon. We got past headaches and each husband told each wife where he really hurt physically. And each wife put her hands where it hurt. I said my prayer aloud and they were invited to say their own to themselves. Then each wife told each husband where she hurt and each husband, with compassion written all over his face, did a laying-on of hands. We broke through boundaries and walls, armor as thick as rage can go, and hit a level of compassion that was as powerful as the rage. It felt as though we had *transformed* the rage into compassion. And by "we" I don't just mean the couples who had lost children and me. I prayed all the way there, I prayed silently as the rage poured out, and we as a group prayed as we helped to heal each other. For many of us that Sunday, we were co-creators with God, co-creating the transformation of hostility and rage into compassion and love.

I was never invited back to that particular group. I never expected to be. I am thankful, though, that I had the opportunity to show this group how to touch again. And I did receive some affirming letters and phone calls.

---

*It is only with the heart that
one can see rightly. What is essential
is invisible to the eye.*

*The Little Prince*
Antoine de Saint-Exupéry

# N I N E

# Divine Energy

For the past ten years I have been a guest speaker in Ken Ring's classes. These are classes specifically for Near-Death Studies, and the students are always bright, articulate and curious. They read *Heading Toward Omega* plus a few other books on altered states, so they're sophisticated when it comes to this subject. That's why I enjoy talking with them and why I don't censor what I'm saying. If they're taking this class, they have to be open-minded or at least curious. So I just talk from my heart.

Not long ago, while doing Ken's class, I was asked to explain what the Holy Spirit is. We had already briefly discussed the physio-Kundalini hypothesis, talked about the energy coming from our hands, healings, etc., and I had switched back and forth many times between the terms Holy Spirit, Kundalini energy, healing energy and Divine Energy. So we had covered quite a bit of ground on the concepts of this energy. Because Kundalini energy is described as more personalized, more the size we are, it is more easily grasped. But the Holy Spirit is talked about with infinite size and qualities. "It's much bigger than our mind is used to picturing, but the quality and action of both are the same," I responded to their question.

I told the students that the most sophisticated descriptions of the Holy Spirit that I have read are throughout the modern holy book *A Course in Miracles.* But while the book describes many of its functions and dimensions in some detail, it is hard to understand without *experiencing* the Holy Spirit directly in our own hearts—in the inner life of our True Self or soul.

I tried to answer the students' question. "You take all the examples of personal feelings of energy, multiply that to cover all of us here on the planet, and connect us to each other and God or the Universe or whatever you're comfortable calling it. Oh! and besides what it feels like, it also has its own intelligence." They looked even more puzzled.

We discussed how these foreign-sounding terms and concepts were confusing, especially given our various ethnic backgrounds. Many in the class, including myself, were born Jewish, and terms like Holy Spirit and Kundalini were far beyond us.[1] Students said they knew the name, but it was only a name. They couldn't conceive of it having a life or an intelligence of its own.

I struggled with what to say next. I took a deep breath and suddenly remembered a wonderful day in early spring many years before when I heard Desmond Tutu speak, about a year after I moved to New England.

## Desmond Tutu and the Holy Spirit

It's time to share this beyond a classroom. It's not a story, really, but an experience that, like so many, is hard to explain

---

[1] Judaism calls this energy *Ruach Ha Kodesh*, The Holy Wind.

because I don't know how to characterize it in words. I'll just have to ask for your cooperation. Read this when you have lots of time and are in a quiet place. Take a deep breath, relax, open your heart and let these words form pictures and feelings that can flow through you.

My first year in research at the University of Connecticut, I lived alone in a small apartment in Hartford. Naively, I had thought of an apartment in the city as romantic, like living in Manhattan. The advertisement for this group of old but stylish and remodeled buildings presented them as not only safe—private security guards—but as the new center for . . . I'm not sure, but it sounded kind of yuppyish and affordable. Anyway, my car had been broken into three times, I had roaches in the Pullman kitchen and there were nightly arrests on the sidewalk in front. The walls between apartments were so thin, I heard everything. But no one was friendly except one man who always said hello, and who, I found out toward the end of my year's lease, was a pimp. Needless to say, I was not a happy inner-city resident! I spent a great deal of time over at my friend Mary Ellen's and we'd talk for hours about the experiences I was studying at UConn. We had Friday night gatherings and this group talked for hours about spirituality, which I really needed. I was having trouble combining my wonderful feelings for the work I was doing and this inner-city lifestyle. My faith was quivering, to say the least!

This new group of friends was primarily Catholic, and often I would hear terms like Holy Spirit and guardian angels. I understood easily that guardian angels were the same or similar to guides or Light beings, but Holy Spirit had me stumped. My new friends would tell me: "Multiply what you feel coming from your hands by a million or more!" and "Remember what it felt like when the breeze wrapped around you in the tunnel."

I was reading and hearing so many descriptions of this energy in my work and at these parties, but my private life was sad and limited. Besides my uncomfortable living situation, I was grieving long and hard from my recent divorce that ended a 22-year marriage. How could I begin to understand the idea of a Holy Spirit?

One Saturday morning in early spring I remember picking up my phone and hearing Dave Doherty, Mary Ellen's brother, say, "Okay, you want to experience the Holy Spirit. This is your chance!"

Disbelieving his words, I asked, "How? What are you talking about! It's Saturday, my day off! I'm going to stay home and read."

"Listen, Barbara," David answered. "If you will ever have a chance to get the Holy Spirit it's this morning and it's happening right around the corner from your apartment. You know the big cathedral on Farmington Avenue? St. Joseph's? Well, Desmond Tutu is scheduled to speak there in about half an hour. Can you be ready in 20 minutes?"

"I'll be ready in 15!" And I was.

Fifteen minutes later I was standing on the curb, watching the traffic, the bag ladies, the kids. A crocus bloomed in the 6-inch strip of dirt between the sidewalk and the building where the last patch of snow was melting. The sun felt good on my face. It felt warm for the first time since what seemed like ages ago. Dave pulled up late and as I jumped in he promised me we'd still get there in time.

As we pulled up to the cathedral, we realized that all the parking lots in the area were full and people were walking from quite a distance. Then a car pulled out from a space directly in front of the cathedral and David yelled, "All right!" and did a quick U-turn in his old Chevy. "Yeah! It's going to be one of those days!"

He grabbed my hand as we ran up—and up—the stairs and into the large foyer, turned right and did a dead stop in front of huge open doors on the extreme right of this magnificent building. Moving toward us was a long procession, four or five people wide. Everyone was dressed in floor-length, brightly-colored robes and tall or square flat hats. Just in front of us they turned and walked down toward the center aisle of the cathedral. A choir sang angelically, trumpets blasted; it was awesome. I was frozen in place. I had never seen anything like this before. It went on and on. Later I heard that there were 200 people in the procession and over 2,000 in the audience.

At the end of the procession, trailing behind, was this little man. He reminded me of a black Barry Fitzgerald. He wore a long red robe with white lace at the collar and cuffs. This was Desmond Tutu. He stopped and looked at a small child in the last pew who was lying there coloring in a book, oblivious to everything. Bishop Tutu began to chat with the child and now he, too, was oblivious to the big scene. Then he rubbed the child's head, patted him on the back and hurried to catch up.

David and I stepped in. There was a low ceiling above us and to the right. To the left where the processional and most of the people sat, the ceiling was so high that I couldn't even guess how many stories up it was. Sunlight streamed in through huge windows. Somewhere behind us to the left there was a balcony with the choir still singing. I couldn't see them and I wanted David to move to the left so we could sit in the big part.

Instead, he moved me to the right and said, "Come on. We may be able to find seats over on the side." I protested, but he let me know we'd be lucky if we could find a place to sit over on the far right, under the low ceiling.

"Oh well," I thought, "I guess we'll just miss the full effect!"

We found seats, folding chairs, way up in the front, all the way over on the right. I stretched and moved around, but could barely see anything that was going on because there was this tall wooden structure obstructing my view. After a few seconds of getting my bearings, I realized it was a pulpit.

I figured I should stop feeling bad because I wasn't in the middle and just sit quietly when Tutu talked. I could close my eyes and concentrate on his words.

Other people talked for a little over an hour. Standing and moving away from my seat for a second, I saw that the main body of the audience was white and well dressed. The 2,000-plus people and the incredibly high ceiling with the sunlight streaming in gave the impression of a tremendous cloud of Light hanging over a massive sea of heads. The small section off to the side where David and I were was filled with most of the blacks who were there.

Finally, they were introducing Tutu. The mass media coverage of the troubles in South Africa had just reached us a few months ago and it was still shocking to hear what was going on. After what seemed like a very long time, the introduction was over and I stretched and squirmed to see where he was. Then I looked up at this pulpit only a few feet away and saw Desmond Tutu standing in it. I was stunned as I looked up and realized he was no farther from me than the length of my own small living room.

## The Power of Prayer

I listened intently. Two thousand other people were perfectly quiet. He wasn't talking about world politics as I thought he would. He was talking about the power of prayer. He said he knew that when enough of us all over the world were praying, there would be relief and peace in South Africa. Whenever he paused, the silence had an awesome quality. Then he lifted his hands up high above his head with his palms raised out flat to the ceiling/sky/heaven and I noticed how tiny his wrists were, encircled in white lace.

"Will you help me?" he said gently. There was total silence.

"Will you help me?" he said with more force, still holding his hands up.

There was a distinct pause, and then one person some-where in the middle of this massive crowd said softly, "Yes."

I think it was David who said next, "Yes!" And then there were scattered shouts from all over. Then the whole crowd was shouting. It became a massive "YES! YES! YES! YES! YES!" over and over.

Over 2,000 people were shouting. There was a palpable wave of energy or wind—something moving through the cathe-dral. The crowd with one voice thundered, "Yes! Yes! Yes!"

At that point David leaned over and said in my ear, "Well, now you have been officially introduced to the Holy Spirit!"

I can't objectively tell you any more . . .

A few minutes later everyone was on their feet, hugging everyone around them. So was I. I thought the black people around me were a little hesitant to hug me, so I did as David did. I grabbed them first and as we embraced we laughed. The laughter sounded as big and as wonderful as the shouts of "Yes" only moments before in St. Joseph's Cathedral. It felt like one giant heart laughing.

David and I spent the rest of the day at Mary Ellen's. We tried to tell her several times what had happened. We could-n't. And I gave up, too, until Ken's class.

Until my spiritual awakening, I was an atheist. As I read back over the manuscript for this book, I relive my own strug-gle to fit the pieces of my journey into a picture that my intel-lect could accept. How does a person not believe in anything one moment and then be flooded with knowing the next? How do you live on dry land and suddenly get swept into a current? Even as I fought against it, and I did at times, it was something more than a memory fighting my intellect. There was this gentle urge at first, which has grown into a living presence that reminds me all the time of Its company.

Call it Chi, Ki, Holy Spirit, Kundalini, Prana, Current of Life or Ruach Ha Kodesh. Be generic and call it bioenergy. The name doesn't matter. It flows through and around us individually and then collectively like an ocean that we all move, breathe and live in. It flows through the Earth and around it and then through and around the other planets, our sun and other solar systems, to form a bigger ocean of living energy. It flows through our galaxy and connects us to other galaxies and on and on.

This energy may be invisible, but it has visible effects. Like a gentle breeze on the surface of a clear peaceful pond, you can see its effects in the changes that we make, in the compassion that we share and by the service that we seek. "By their fruits you shall know them."[2]

After my spiritual awakening there was my need to help others. When I started volunteering in the emergency room, it was my head that was relieved of pain when the energy ran out of my hands to the old woman who was so sick. She got better, at least for a little while, and so did I. All the work, therapy and education that I have continued to seek out is for my own need to grow and to know what is real. A byproduct of the transformational journey has been helping other people. This was at the urging and guidance of this formless energy that I would love to prove exists, and can't. All I can do is be with It, work with It and be thankful for It when my heart fills to overflowing.

## Music of the Energy

About six years ago I met Joel Funk, a professor of psychology from Plymouth State College, when he came to visit Bruce and me at the University of Connecticut and talk about his research into music and the near-death experience. I excitedly told him about "The Angels of Comfort" from the tape called "Angelic Music." About five years earlier, I had heard this piece of music that contained what I had heard in the tunnel during my NDE, while this gentle breeze caressed

_____
[2] Matthew 7:20.

me and I watched the darkness churning, separating, and Light coming from darkness. I told Joel that I had described the sound as a low droning noise until I listened and meditated to this certain piece and realized what it was.

Recently I sat in on a workshop Joel gave at the New England IANDS Conference, and he played "The Angels of Comfort" for the participants. Over the last several years he has played this music with several other modern and classical pieces for several large groups of experiencers, plus control groups, in a scientific study. This musical composition was chosen to most closely represent our spiritual experiences: for those of us who heard sound during our NDE, it is the closest to what we heard or exactly what we heard.

At the end of the workshop Joel read parts of a letter from Iasos, the composer, replying to Joel's inquiry about the music. Iasos said that he had asked specifically for the energy of the Holy Spirit to assist him and he had asked straight from his heart. Iasos wrote:

To summarize the creation of The Angels of Comfort, I reached a point in my ability to manifest music, where I realized that anything I can imagine, I can create. There has never been any music that I could imagine but could not create. In contemplating this wonderful thought, I then thought: "In that case, what music would I like to create, if I can create ANY music?" I decided that I wanted to create music that had the energy of the Holy Spirit in it. So I went within, and silently but sincerely made a mental request: "Oh Holy Spirit, I wish to create music that has your energy in it. Please assist me in creating music that has your essence in it."

To my great surprise, as quickly as one week later, some musician friends allowed me to use a synthesizer that sounded like many violins (something I myself did not then have). I quickly went into their studio, set up my recorder, recorded feverishly for two and a half hours, and then they returned and informed me my time was up. I said thank you very much. I went home to my studio with that recording, experimented pressing what I had recorded, and to my great surprise realized that a composition of great beauty and depth was emerging— The Angels of Comfort. It sounded very composed, although at the time I was recording, I was not thinking of any particular composition. After the piece materialized, it became abundantly clear that this was the answer to my request from the Holy Spirit.

In my understanding, the Holy Spirit is not something mythical related only to the Christian church. . . . One of the functions of the Holy Spirit is to grant comfort to all souls. . . . The Holy Spirit, furthermore, is directly involved in participating in every death and every birth that occurs on this planet. It is no surprise then, that this music of the Holy Spirit, The Angels of Comfort, is often selected as music to be used at births, at deaths, and selected by NDErs as similar to what they heard.

So the sound that I heard in my NDE was the sound of the Holy Spirit or Kundalini, Divine Energy, whatever we chose to call it. And the gentle breeze I felt is the feeling of the same energy. The Light separating from the darkness that I saw in the tunnel is the action of this intelligent force and it's still acting this way every day in my life and in all our lives— the Light outshining the darkness—intelligence guiding us in our growth.

I know of no one who rationally resisted this as much as I did, even when the Universe was being blatant. However, I was bombarded so often with cosmic greeting cards that logic just had to give in!

Finally I said, "All right! All right!"

## Joy

Not too long after hearing Desmond Tutu, I experienced ecstatic joy for the first time. I remember being terrified that I would burn up or something awful would happen to me because I didn't know joy well or its effects. So I was afraid to experience it. "What should I do?" I asked Mary Ellen in a slightly panicked voice.

She laughed. "You're always asking God and the energy of the Holy Spirit to help you in your healings. Why not ask the Holy Spirit now to take the spillover from your joy? Give some back. The Holy Spirit is always your partner. It will be more than happy to be your partner in joy!"

I tried it and it worked. Now, whenever something wonderful is happening or whenever I feel even faintly afraid, I think of this energy as my partner. Then I feel it, then I ask. Reality to me now is a dance of energies. Through these energies each of us is connected to our experiences, to each other and to God. To embrace this dance, to see the divine in everything, is to become vulnerable to the flows of feelings created by this energy, feelings that are quite non-rational and can create complete peace and ecstatic joy when we finally let go into the harmony.

I used to be a hard-nosed atheist with a scientific background. And now—I won't mince words—I am a Practical Mystic having this wonderful love affair with a breeze that I can't see or prove but that has impeccable timing and is certainly wiser than I.

## T E N

# Spiritual Sexuality

his chapter is not only about sex; it's also about spirituality and commune-ication in psychologically mature intimate relationships. It's about spiritual beings having a human experience.

Originally, I became aware of a shift in attitude and experience in sex when I started lecturing. Women confided after my talks that they'd had some kind of spiritual awakening and then experienced what can be summed up as Divine Energy shared in lovemaking. Or their spiritual awakening happened during lovemaking and was preceded by this rush of energy. I was fortunate to have been able to talk later with their intimate partners, who confirmed these reports and shared the other side of spiritual sex.[1] Now I bring up spiritual and tran-

---

[1] Also, I've had many audience participants and other speakers tell me of periods in their journey where they wanted celibacy. The time

scendent sexual experiences in my talks, explaining them as a way of having a spiritual experience, and audience participants ask questions and add knowledge from their own experiences.

In achieving this type of lovemaking, there is an energetic bonding that demands future respect. Without loyalty, these experiences can destroy a relationship. I'm not advocating that spiritual sex should replace Western sex, but it is an option that we can experience occasionally, either through spontaneously desiring it or planned as a ritual to celebrate the intimate relationship we have with each other and the Universe. In other words, it is an intimate sharing of primal and Divine Energy that bonds, and shouldn't be overdone or taken lightly. In the spirit of celebrating the love between two mature adults, it bonds them to each other and to the Universe.

Over the last ten years, I have heard beautiful ecstatic accounts of lovemaking from both women and men. They reported the same psychological, psychophysical and spiritual aftereffects I have described in this book. Because of the spiritual nature of these accounts, all approached and shared without any inhibition or embarrassment. Being psychologically and spiritually mature, we know it is time to share this with our brothers and sisters who are also spiritual beings learning to have a human experience.[2]

## Our Nature

Spirituality and sexuality are the two sides of one coin, the coin being our nature. One side is physical. Its nature is

span I've heard, and practiced myself, is a year or two. For some it becomes a permanent choice.

[2] Psychological and spiritual maturity is defined here in terms of Whitfield's recovery stages, described in his foreword. Those completing Stage Two and who feel comfortable in Stage Three are probably ready for this deep intimacy. For those individuals who jumped to Stage Three without doing the psychological healing of Stage Two (spiritual bypass), this new form of intimate relationship will not likely work long-term. I warn of this hazard several times in this chapter. The false self, or negative ego, will usually be energized by this type of sharing, and negativity will commonly result.

innocent and earthy. This means we can express ourselves in uninhibited free sex. This doesn't mean that we have a different partner every night. That's sexual addiction. I'm talking about letting our bodies take over and express themselves without our minds getting in the way. The other side of the coin, the other side of our nature, is *spiritual*. Humans crave their spiritual nature, the direct experience of spirit. We have a natural ability to directly experience spirit through our bodies, just as we were meant to express our earthy, innocent side through our bodies, too.

Sex is about surrendering to our body's natural instincts to move and be what it wants in this perfect moment. Our body wants to be in the now. We want to lose our minds and gain our senses. Sex is also about surrendering to our body's spiritual instincts, to not move and be what it is in this Holy Moment. And sexuality is a key. It is a doorway to the higher realms of transcendent consciousness.

## The Path of Intimate Relationship

On the threshold of the millennium we approach the next peak in our evolution. As more and more people awaken to their spiritual nature and heal their True Selves, history will write its first chapter of authentic human selfhood experienced in mass numbers. Those who have patiently worked hard to transform will seek intimate relationships with other healthy people or heal the relationships they already have.[3] Our evolution will quicken again from these sacred and secure relationships. However, because we have no past experience to fall back on, we realize we are standing on uncharted ground. Now we want, need and desire with all our hearts to have relationships that are different. We are different and we want to be who we are with someone who is also whole and can share authentically.

---

[3] Read Whitfield's *Co-dependence: Healing the Human Condition.*

We desire to be fully ourselves and be with someone who will honor our individuality and whom we can trust. At the same time, we have a need to let go of centering on our self and lose ourselves to our partner. The paradox is scary. We must be able to be authentic and stand our ground, and, at the same time, let go. Being genuinely present and intimate with another person forces us to live on the edge of the unknown. As John Welwood says, "We dance on the razor's edge where we feel vulnerable, sharply pierced by our need to love and be loved." Yet we need to feel pierced in this way or we won't be capable of the kind of love that we have intuited is possible. We need to discover and learn to dance in the shakiness of love's great balancing act. Then we also learn to dance with the flux and change continually occurring in all our relationships. By balancing back and forth we find a new equilibrium. We come to realize that an alive relationship is continually going in and out of balance. Each moment of uncertainty indicates different aspects of ourselves and/or the other trying to come into balance. We can only discover how to proceed in these moments by daring to feel, acknowledging both sides and seeing where that leads.[4]

Of course, balancing on the razor's edge, being fully present with another person without holding on to any formula or strategy, is still scary. However, the fear and rawness we feel when we have nothing to hold onto from past experience indicate that we are on our growing edge. Every time my partner and I start to feel disconnected, this spurs us to explore and talk about what is happening between us. This can help us to connect again, often in a new and richer way.[5] When there is conflict and it is resolved, deeper levels of intimacy result. We learn from experience that conflict does not have to lead to abuse. Conflict can be fertile ground for the

---

[4] Welwood, *The Healing Power of Unconditional Presence.*
[5] Ibid.

discovery of new areas in our self, our partner and our relationship. Learning to trust this process helps us to live more and more with ambiguity. Patiently learning to trust this process ripens the relationship to a level of companionship and friendship perhaps unknown to us before.

Intimacy involves a sharing in the spirit of desiring to be known and to know more about one another. Anything that is shared can serve to enhance the relationship. Trust develops by sharing our innermost thoughts and feelings gradually and seeing how they are received. True trust is *felt*, not *willed*. It's a feeling that develops gradually over time through this process of sharing.

It is also important to be able to risk asking for help, acknowledging vulnerability in occasionally feeling helpless. During many moments of our journey, we may have felt painfully lonely and then turned that feeling into the more neutral one of being alone, and finally into the positive sense of being independent. Now that we have achieved healthy independence, it is time to practice occasionally leaning on another person in a healthy dependent way. This then invites the other person to lean on us when needed.

The most difficult ongoing task is to watch for and prevent projections from our past relationships.[6] It's necessary to clear the negativities surrounding our sexuality. We get to see our present partner instead of projecting a previous relationship onto this present one. Not projecting, we are no longer living in the past and are better able to be in the joy of the present moment.

As all of the above ways are experienced by two people who have offered themselves to each other in intimate relationship, deeper levels of fear can dissolve. This loss of fear is crucial to intimacy and spiritual sexuality. We can finally abandon the fear of what our partner may think of us during

---

[6] See *Healing the Child Within* or *Co-dependence*.

lovemaking. "That's not the way nice girls behave," or "I'm not supposed to feel this way," or "I've got to perform to satisfy her" may be thoughts that walled us off in the past from being in our bodies. Now we no longer hear those old tapes in our inner life. Or if we do, we are aware of them and can let them go. We can be in our bodies so completely that our mind need not negotiate anything. Then we may move in complete abandonment not only in sex, but in every facet of our relationship. And we may also *not* move in complete abandonment. We can abandon the fear of what our partner may think of the way we are all the time. We can move and be uninhibited as if we are alone—only now we *share* our alone time.

The path of intimate relationships may not be for everyone. It may even be inappropriate for some or in some situations. The rewards, however, include personal growth, authenticity, personal freedom and a sense of fulfillment. The prerequisite is courage to risk by two whole people.

## Before and Beyond Words

Throughout this book I have suggested opening to possibilities that are beyond words, sometimes talking about primal senses or higher sense perceptions, other times using metaphors to try to describe concepts that stretch our imagination beyond words. Much of what I have shared is so mystical that it is not contained in ordinary physical reality. I hope this has prepared us for a discussion of the type of loving intimate relationship that my intuition told me existed, and that I am now dancing with myself. The dance begins when we move into the emotionality of the moment by experiencing our feelings rather than just the sexual stimulation of the body.

Telepathic abilities and other higher sense perceptions give new possibilities to our deepening experience of love. The love we share with our intimate partner no longer needs to be expressed primarily through words or language, but through the quality of one's presence, one's being. As our language-based culture makes room for the emergence of telepathic possibilities, our ability to experience love deepens. Words are still important. Nothing can ever replace "I love you." But with or without words, we can now experience greater intensity and depth in loving. In a few brief moments all the words can disappear and we feel our joining with the other. The possibilities between two spiritual beings having a human experience are limitless. No longer is it the two of us. Sometimes we feel as one. Other times the larger spiritual Presence is felt. Divine Energy makes itself known personally. Two then understand and experience the sacred three (God, you and me) becoming One. We are not only sharing this healing energy in selfless service to others, but now it makes Its Presence known with our intimate partner in love.

## We Are One

My sense is that before God created us, there was no polarity. God has no gender, no separate Yin and Yang energy. God is before the split, polarity or duality. Because we appear separate, every time we get closer to God we therefore experience more paradox. Our split brain, left and right, can't reconcile this paradox. Only experiencing union with God heals the split. But this union is not an intellectual decision. Our spiritual awakenings show us that union with God is a direct personal experience. Prayer and meditation can continue to confirm the union, and may have even connected us the first time. Sexuality connects us into a frequency of ecstasy that then connects us back to our Divine Source.

When two share, or join energy in spiritual sex or even in just holding each other,[7] they unite the split and feel a deep oneness. Their separately polarized energies join and form the one energy again. The energetic tension that is usually felt

---

[7] I have also heard reports of these experiences happening while being held, regardless of sexual preference.

subtly between the two lovers when not joined can transform into a balancing of the energy, back to its original form, Unity. God can know Godself through the union of opposites. When we share the charged energy until it merges and equalizes, creating oneness, we are co-creating with God. Opposite ends of the polarity melt, bonding into a balanced continuum. Peacefulness and clarity result. Over the next several days the tension or charge builds and is again transformed in the next celebration of loving sex I am about to describe.

## The Action of Spiritual Sex

To comprehend this type of union we can think in subtle terms, terms before words, and action unlike the type of sex we have practiced here in the West. The action of spiritual sex has practically no action. It is a *being with* and a *letting be.* It uses the same level of sensitivity as in a healing or a telepathic communication. It is as in meditation, breathing in a relaxed manner but also occasionally focusing on the subtle feelings at the point of contact. Eventually, this point may radiate through our bodies, a higher sense perception acting in the most primal way.

The sense of reverence or sacredness that we have felt in other ways may now be revealed for our selves and for our partner. We also realize that as subtle as this shared energy is, as gentle as its stream feels, that is how powerful its effects are. It creates new paths for the energy, which in its emotional component is unconditional love. The creation of these new paths burns through blocks, as described in the chapters on Kundalini. If the false self, or ego, is still in control of us, this spiritual energy will operate to dissolve it. The ego will react as if it is being attacked, or at the least being threatened, not necessarily during sex, but sometime after. If both people in an intimate relationship have their True Selves in charge of their life, this type of union is appropriate. And if not, they may want to wait until later.[8]

## Letting Go

NDErs talk about the moment of letting go, of surren... to their death scene and then the NDE starting. Effective meditators experience that surrender of control every time they meditate. So do biofeedback experiencers and athletes when they move into a peak-performance state. Athletes will describe such altered states of consciousness as runner's high, with a sense of their bodies flowing with the moment and spirit moving in and merging during the experience. On both sides of our nature, spiritual and physical, we surrender or let go and let whatever we are doing, do us. Singers talk about the song singing them. The feeling is one of freeing ourselves to be ourselves. So it is with sexual spiritual wholeness. If one lets one's body move or rest freely while concentrating on the direct perception of feelings and sensations, this will happen naturally.

Wilhelm Reich, psychoanalyst and natural scientist, recognized that "People who are connected to their energy, including their sexuality and their passion, are in tune with the divine, for expressing the inherently loving side of human nature is the core of unfeigned spirituality." Reich said that making love is humankind's attempt to return to the original, unimpeded flow of cosmic energy.

During lovemaking we need to forget about our training, our beliefs and our spirituality. We simply are there with the moment as we are in meditation or centering.

## The Three Elements of Transcendence

Three basic elements are experienced when we come into the blissful moment. First, we *transcend time*. Time ceases to exist. As in our spiritual awakenings, there is no past and,

---

[8] One who is still living from the false self may have trouble understanding this concept.

future. This moment becomes the only real moment. Second, we *transcend the ego*. We and our beloved are completely lost into something else. And third, we are *totally natural*. We are a part of nature, as a tree or a flower or a bird. We are also in something greater, the Universe. We are floating in it. We are taken by the current. These three things give us the ecstasy. Sex is just a situation in which it happens naturally. Once we have experienced these three elements in sex we can also experience them in meditation, or vice versa.

In 1949, Rudolf von Urban, M.D., wrote *Sexual Perfection and Marital Happiness*. Von Urban was a general practitioner and a psychotherapist. He recommended this type of sex to couples to rekindle love. Brave and ahead of his time, he said:

> This may be an over-simplification, but let me explain . . . No one can attain the goal of sex perfection unless he [sic] possesses or acquires certain qualities of character. Chief among these are unselfishness, honesty, reliability and emotional maturity, which means development from the state of taking to the state of giving.
>
> I do not advance this doctrine on religious or ethical grounds, but purely from the psychological point of view. A person whose character has developed in this way is at peace with himself; his energies are not dissipated in battles with his more or less unconscious feelings of guilt; he does not waste time on self-reproach. How necessary the state of relaxation is to the achievement of sex perfection I hope to make clear. . . . If both partners are cooperative—it is my business to see that they are—and if no outsider interferes, the miracle happens, their love is re-born.
>
> When this is done, and full sex satisfaction is attained, their old love for each other returns in full force; indeed it is often deeper and truer love than before. During my 45 years of practice I have become convinced of the important part which sex satisfaction plays in molding the marriage relationship. Real sex satisfaction leads inevitably

to a deep feeling of love; and with love and patience, faulty traits of character can be corrected. . . .

True, the science of sex cannot be grasped in a day, but anyone who wants to, and who will persist, can attain this goal. Such mastery will not only bring incalculable benefits to the lives of the next generation, but will also add immeasurably to the happiness of adults today.

What these experiences have in common is a gentle quality, where one or both of the partners feel a beautiful energy shared in a closed circuit between them, dipping into an altered state containing a sense of peace, tranquility and connection to the divine. Similar to meditation, they remain in this relaxed state while connected genitally, with no thrusting movement except if the erection is being lost. If the erection is being lost, then there is gentle thrusting until there is enough erection to continue penetration. Full erection is not necessary. Both partners should lie at right angles to each other, the woman on her back with one leg between the man's thighs and the other leg resting on his hip. In this way the contact is purely genital and the whole relationship between the two pours through this center. While this is a good way to begin in this experience, there is no need to make it a fixed rule.

There is usually no talking, because that creates a disturbance. This union becomes as peaceful as the surface of a pond with no breeze. Here we don't use our minds at all. We use our bodies. The mind is only used to sense what is happening. We don't think; we just feel the warmth that is flowing, the love that is flowing, the energy that is in contact. Be aware of it. And all of this should not be a strain—rather, in it we are effortlessly floating. Only then, after a while, in "no time" the valley will appear. And once the valley appears, transcendence happens. Once the valley is realized—the relaxed orgasm—transcendence is already achieved. Sex is no longer there. *Now* it is a meditation of peaceful ecstasy.

## Comparison of Peak and Valley Orgasm[9]

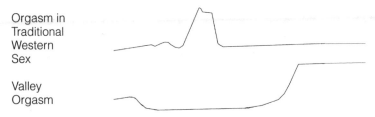

Orgasm in
Traditional
Western
Sex

Valley
Orgasm

The orgasm in this experience is totally different from traditional Western sex, which is always thought of as a peak or burst, or throwing off of the energy. If that is a peak, then this is a valley, a long peaceful pause deepening into a transcendent peaceful ecstasy. We do not reach the peak of excitement, but come into the very deepest valley of relaxation. There is only excitement in the beginning, for the man to enter. But once the man has entered, both lover and beloved can relax. No movement is needed. They can relax in a loving embrace, or just the genitals need touch. Meditation or centering is then all that is needed. If no other parts of the body are touching, the current felt deep within the point of contact will be subtle and apparent, sooner and easier.

When the couple come out of the valley orgasm, they maintain the sense of peace and quiet joy that they experienced while connected. Usually the sense remains until the next encounter. This is a peaceful surrendering that brings us back a little higher and more joyful than when we started, as shown on the right of the figure. According to von Urban, the energy cycle becomes apparent and the bliss sets in at about 28 minutes, then continues for a prolonged period. All whom I have spoken with say that it happens sooner and that there

---

[9] The orgasmic sensations are no longer exclusively dependent on genital interaction but are often perceived as an altered state of consciousness (Anand).

is a timeless quality that transcends worrying about the clock. Regular meditation lasts about 20 minutes or a little longer. Spiritual sex seems about the same. What does change, however, is our sense of vitality, a feeling of being younger and livelier. When we meet with our beloved in such a relaxed state, our energy is renewed. The realizations that accompany these experiences may be expanding, but start with:

Transcendence doesn't come through friction and conflict—It comes through tension, letting go and awareness!

E L E V E N

# Embracing Soul, Inviting Spirit

For those who have awakened spiritually or those who want to, here are exercises and ideas to help you open and remain open. Remember, with each one the element of letting go or surrender is the beginning and continuous mind-set.

We let go all the time. We let go every time we fall in love. And falling in love for us is not a rare occurrence. We fall in love whenever we give ourselves to someone or something: with people, causes, objects, activities, beliefs and experiences. If this seems difficult for you, just remember:

> What had been judgment and control can, with a little space and Grace, become appreciation and wonder.[1]

---

[1] Gerald May, 1991.

## In Prayer

Prayer can be anything from reciting words by rote, to pleading for help in desperation, to simple appreciation in the present moment. My prayers are me talking to myself and to God. When overwhelmed with good things in my life, sometimes I walk around saying "Thank you, thank you!" and the thank-yous are prayers coming from my heart. The fullness in my heart is almost overwhelming. The thank-you I send with prayerful sincerity alleviates the pressure and helps me to accept these gifts without fear. I have been told many times that prayers of gratitude are the best prayers of all.

Practical Mystics know that Grace is a gift. We can neither earn it nor make it happen. Grace invites us to participate. It needs our involvement. So when we know Grace is needed, prayer is the one way we may possibly bring it in.

I have learned over the years that when praying, be very specific and then visualize what you are requesting. Visualize it exactly as you want it to happen. *Intend* it to happen. Intention can be a lightning rod. Also, make absolutely sure that you are ready for what you are asking. This is a time when it is really important to know your own inner life. Are you having any inner resistance?

I have seen prayer work in my life and the lives of my loved ones over and over again. We all agree that when prayer brings special moments of Grace, love is everywhere, our very life becomes a prayer.

## Finding a Heart Prayer

This idea from *The Awakened Heart* by Gerald May, M.D. involves selecting a word, phrase or image and planting it deeply within yourself during times of prayer and meditation. Then, during the rest of the day, notice it going on inside in the midst of all your activities.

The deepest way of finding a heart prayer is to ask God to give it to you. It will then emerge from your heart and represents the deep, wordless prayer that has been going on inside you all along. To use Brother Lawrence's words, "let love inspire it." Just make the request and then be still, watching for what seems to be given: a word, phrase, image or feeling that comes into your awareness spontaneously.

If something comes and has a right kind of feeling about it, do not worry about whether it has been divinely inspired or whether you have conjured it up yourself. Caress it a little. Does it deepen your presence or pull you away? Does it inspire trust or fear? Does it represent love or alienation, willingness or willfulness? If it doesn't seem right, go back to your Source and ask to return it in exchange for another. Ask yourself to remember this word or image through the day. And in the evening, just before you fall asleep, meditate on it for a few minutes. Keep this going for one or even two weeks and when you feel ready, ask for a new heart prayer.

## In Nature

While just being—this means not doing—somewhere outdoors in a natural setting, ask to form a relationship with your surroundings primarily through reverence, awe and wonder. Remember the Divine Presence in all things. Notice evidences of it, the pulse of creation, the love it has taken to complete all the details. Stretch your heart open while keeping your feet firmly planted. Welcome and join the living flow of love. It is giving oneself into the Mystery and allowing the mystery of oneself to participate in endless graceful surprise. Welcome the presence without trying to identify or label it. Welcome mystery into yourself; look for awe; recover childlike wonder.[2]

---

[2] May

## Stairway to the Stars

During my second or third year in research at the University of Connecticut I was given—this was Grace—the opportunity to live in a beach house on Long Island Sound. It was no ordinary beach house. The rumor was that it had been built by the family of Frank Lloyd Wright, and it was still possible to see his type of design in this huge old place that had been divided into four apartments. I had the upstairs that had once been the master suite. The front of it jutted out over the water, so while inside, the all-glass view was over the water as though you were on the back of a ship. The side wall, again all glass, looked back at the shoreline for as far as the eye could see because we were out on a point. It was incredible—and out of season, so I could afford the rent. I lived there for eight months.

I drove an hour each way to the university but I didn't care! The first night that I came home to my new place, the roar of the waves crashing against the rocks drew me to the sea wall. I stood there in the ink-black darkness trying to let my eyes become accustomed to the night without city lights. I had never been in such darkness before. The waves were roaring and crashing, invading my mind with such a fullness there was no room for words. I looked up into the night sky and felt blasted in a way I had never known before. My body cowered and I pulled the hood of my jacket over my head for fear of shooting into the Universe and losing my self. I stayed for as long as I could tolerate the Power and then ran to the outdoor wood staircase that led up to my second-story deck. It ascended in the same direction as the seawall, and I was now in the same view but higher. I took my hood off, breathed in the cool salt air and looked up again, feeling reverence and gratitude for the wonder of it all and my participation in it.

Every evening, for eight months, I ascended my Stairway to the Stars. I would pause at the same spot and catch a glimpse of the Mystery and honor my participation.

I have heard many other profound experiences from people visiting Findhorn in Scotland, the Great Pyramids of Egypt, or The Wailing Wall in Israel. Here in the United States we have Sedona, Arizona; Muir Woods, north of San Francisco; Native American kivas (temples); the Colorado mountains; the Lincoln Memorial; and the list goes on and on.

I have also heard of profound experiences from participants of wilderness trainings and shamanic initiations.

## In Dreams

Have you ever had a lucid dream? Most of us have had at least one experience of realizing that we're dreaming even while in the midst of a dramatic adventure or terrifying threat. At that moment we become *lucid*—we are dreaming yet we know that we are dreaming. That moment can result in a sense of relief, delight, wonder and freedom. We are then free to confront our monsters, fulfill our desires or seek our highest goals, knowing we are creators, not victims of our experiences.[3]

At the moment we dreamers wake, or become lucid, in a dream, we are offered a wonderful metaphor for enlightenment. In that moment of awakening we are startled to recognize that what formerly seemed an unquestionably objective, material and independent world is in fact an internal, subjective, immaterial and dependent mental creation and that we are the creators, not the victims of the dream.[4] Then we can easily invite God or the spiritual into our dream and experience the numinous consciously. This can easily, and usually does if we ask, carry over into our waking life. Lucid dreaming has been recommended for hundreds of years by Yogic, Sufi and Tibetan Buddhist traditions. Until the 1970s, Western psychologists dismissed it as impossible.

[3] Walsh, 1993.
[4] Walsh, *Revisions Journal*.

If you would like to investigate this, books and workshops on lucid dreaming have become increasingly popular. You can then actively seek within the dream for a spiritual experience. Then let go and turn control of the dream over to a Higher Power, whether it is conceived to be an inner guide, Divine Energy or God. Seek to remain continuously aware during your dreams.[5]

The request you can make to yourself in prayer, in meditation and when falling asleep can be something like: "Next time I'm dreaming, I want to recognize I'm dreaming."

Steven LaBerge, lucid-dream researcher and author of *Lucid Dreaming* and *The World of Lucid Dreaming,* spells out the intention step by step:

> 1.  During the early morning, when you awaken spontaneously from a dream, go over the dream several times until you have memorized it.
> 2.  Then, while lying in bed and returning to sleep, say to yourself, "Next time I'm dreaming, I want to remember to recognize I'm dreaming."
> 3.  Visualize yourself as being back in the dream just rehearsed; only this time, see yourself realizing that you are, in fact, dreaming.
> 4.  Repeat steps two and three until you feel your intention is clearly fixed or you fall asleep.

It took me about two weeks of the above steps and I started waking up in my dreams. Here's an example of one of my first conscious moments of waking in a dream.

> I am standing on the shore of a river. My seven-year-old son is being tied to me. The back of his head is just below my chin and I can feel my heart beating fast against his back. Ropes are wrapped around our chests, waists and hips. We are pushed into the water. I realize that he is under and unable to breathe. I start treading

---

[5] Walsh, 1993.

the water as hard and as fast as I can. His face is above water now and we are moving. I am propelling us by swimming and treading in an upright position so he can breathe. There is some turbulence. We can't swim directly across the river to the other shore. I am struggling and feeling myself weakening. As I continue fighting the current, I am exhausted and let go. I wake up in the dream and ask for God's help. As I "let go" we move down the river and then the current takes us back up to the other side. There are friendly people there waiting to pull us out. They untie the ropes and we are helped into the back of a convertible. My child sits on my lap and we are driven to a beautiful city with mystical looking buildings. People are cheering for us. We are being given a hero's welcome.

## Transpersonal Psychotherapy

A transpersonal psychotherapist considers caring for the soul as well as the psychological well-being of the client in therapy. This orientation does not invalidate other approaches, but expands their context to include our spiritual nature. Transpersonal psychotherapy is presumed to be more suitable for relatively healthy, growth-oriented clients. Psychiatrists, psychologists and other psychotherapists receive additional training about transpersonal issues and much of this training is experiential, so they are usually on a psychospiritual journey, too. According to Frances Vaughan in her book, written with Roger Walsh, *Paths Beyond Ego,* there are many methods commonly associated with transpersonal therapy and they may be applied at any level of development. They can be used to assist us to open to inner experiences. Some of them are:

—Body work, such as breath and body work, bioenergetics, hatha-yoga, t'ai chi, aikido, chi gong, biofeedback, sensory awareness and movement therapy, to name just a few. These disciplines train awareness on subtle physical sensations and some focus specifically on mind-body integration.

—Emotional catharsis. The release of emotional blocks is essential for healing the wounds of the past and freeing a person to live fully in the present. Some methods are: individual or group therapy with a transpersonal-oriented psychotherapist, breath work, breath and body work together, guided imagery and dream work. One of the most effective methods for emotional catharsis is holotropic breathing, developed by Stanislav and Christina Grof.

—Imagery and dream work: dream analysis, active imagination, Gestalt dialogue and the hypnotic induction of altered states. Transpersonal work does not depend on the technique, but on how it is used. Do not be afraid to ask a therapist before trying a particular method about spiritual issues and transpersonal training.

—Confession. A transpersonal therapist provides a relationship that can include a contemporary version of the confessional for many people who have become alienated from formal religion. This can provide a safe place where the darkest secret places in the psyche are accepted and reintegrated into a larger vision of wholeness.[6]

—Adult-Child Recovery offers us the opportunity to heal our old wounds and to then realize more fully our own authenticity. If there is child abuse or trauma in our background, this work is a *solid foundation* that will support our spiritual growth.[7]

## Choosing a Therapist or Spiritual Teacher

Whenever visiting a therapist of any kind, the rule is—Don't be afraid to ask about the therapist's training or philosophy. Some types of training may have come from a one-weekend workshop. Others take years of study. An example could be past-life regression. Weekend workshops claim to teach this method. My guide was a Ph.D. clinical

---

[6] Vaughan, 1993.
[7] Whitfield, *Co-dependence*, 1991.

psychologist whom I had faith in because he also had many years of psychological training and had experienced and learned everything offered on past-life therapy. This possibility of too brief a training period also applies to rebirthing, hypnosis, positive thinking, affirmations, etc.

As noted in the section on finding a teacher to learn psychic abilities—in chapter 8—talk to other people who have experienced what you are going to do with the therapist or guide you are going to use. Would they go back? Then, what is your gut feeling about this method and especially this therapist, friend or spiritual teacher/guide who is offering it?

A final word: I have heard sad and destructive stories of short- and long-term affairs between spiritual teachers and students, and between therapists and clients. This is sexual abuse and *should never happen.*

Charles Whitfield, in *A Gift to Myself,* writes:

> There is another important kind of transference that is fairly common, especially in individual counseling or therapy, and that is becoming infatuated with our therapist.
>
> Rather than being "true love," this "positive" transference nearly always means that we are projecting onto the therapist or other helping professional many of the healing qualities that we have already inherent within ourself, but we do not know that we do.
>
> This kind of transference is potentially dangerous. Not only can it block our healing, but if a therapist breaks their ethical code and gets into any kind of physical and/or emotional "affair" with us, the wheels are now in motion for us to be further mistreated and wounded. Aside from being unethical practice by the therapist, this may have the devastating effect of discouraging us from all future attempts at psychospiritual growth.
>
> To help prevent these dangerous consequences and to protect ourselves, we can risk talking about it with our therapist when even the first hint of it comes up.
>
> The therapist or counselor—or helping professional of any kind—should be trained to recognize and to deal with this positive transference in a way that is most healing to

you. In this situation you are vulnerable. Before any such "affair," or even a hint of one, and before any of these other destructive consequences, it is the responsibility of the therapist to use this transference to assist you in working through any associated conflicts and in discovering your own inner strengths.

You can trust nearly all therapists to be ethical, responsible, and to safely facilitate your work through the real conflict underneath the transference. Probably less than 5 percent of therapists are themselves unhealed in this kind of situation. Rather than facilitate your healing work through the transference, they may—coming from their countertransference or from simple lust—try to initiate a physical and/or emotional affair with you. But there is never a justification for doing that. It will inevitably damage you.

Some people who may be especially vulnerable to being mistreated or abused by their therapist in this way are those who have been physically or sexually abused as children, adolescents or even as adults, and others who have *blurred* personal boundaries.

If you come close to having such an affair, it is then healing to find a safe person with whom to talk about and process your experience. While you may be reluctant to do so, at this point it can be constructive to search out a new therapist.

Whenever spiritual growth is involved, our hearts are open. If you are learning from a spiritual teacher, many times these teachers have little or no training, but have evolved into their position because of a heart chakra opening and subsequent spiritual experiences. However, if their lower chakras—emotional and sexual development—are not balanced the relationship could become seductively charged. As I described in the section on romantic projection, whenever a heart relationship—teaching relationship as well as friendship—becomes physical/sexual, ego feelings such as anger, jealousy, shame, guilt, etc., will be activated in a powerful way. The best action is *no* action. And finding a safe person to talk with. Affairs with spiritual teachers or guides are not about psychospiritual growth. They are about abuse!

## Altered States of Consciousness

The use of techniques such as music, fasting, drumming, chanting, dancing and ingesting drugs to alter consciousness is as old as recorded history. Altered states can have powerful therapeutic effects and for those I have interviewed, the aftereffects are as powerful as any I have described. With or without an experience, altered states facilitate the process of awakening by enhancing inner awareness and intuition.

## Spontaneous Ritual

Ritual and prayer combined with life's great moments such as childbirth, can invite an experience. Ritual before lovemaking can do the same. Make up a ritual for any time that has meaning for you. Let go of preconceived beliefs and let it happen.

### Our Rutgers Experience

On the last morning of a one-week course on spirituality for counselors and therapists that I was co-teaching, one student offered our class for a closing ceremony a bottle of holy water she had brought from the River Jordan. She told us she had taken it from the spot where Jesus had been baptized. We hadn't thought about a closing ritual until she brought it up this last hour of class. I had my Sabbath candles in my dorm room because I was staying over on Friday evening, and offered to share my Jewish ritual of blessing the Sabbath candles. We all agreed. As I lit them saying a Hebrew prayer, the students circled around and then we were each blessed with the holy water. There was an outpouring of joy. We have remembered that moment every time we see each other on subsequent years at Rutgers School of Alcohol and Drug

Studies. I have heard tear-filled joyful memories from the other students in the class; some contain elements of transcendent spiritual awakenings.

## Circle of Forgiveness

Here is a personal ritual that I do in my own meditations. It is a combination of guided imagery and prayer.

After taking several cleansing breaths I then move through my body, asking each part to relax. I then invite God and the loving energy of the Holy Spirit to join with me in creating a circle of forgiveness. I see myself in a meadow in the middle of a forest. I take a stick and draw a big circle in the grass. I stand outside the circle and think about those I need to forgive. I notice what is coming up for me: self-pity, sense of being a victim, loss of integrity, etc. I ask God and the energy of the Holy Spirit to take these painful feelings away. I make a commitment to continue as I feel these painful feelings lift. I step into the circle and call in the person I need to forgive.

I tell these people what they have done to me. I am blunt, straightforward. I let go, hold nothing back. I can show my emotion, cry, scream or even cheer if I feel my own strength coming back to me.

Then I move 90 degrees clockwise and so do they. Now I can talk about how I feel about myself: naive, embarrassed, humiliated. I talk about how I have punished myself over all this. I can also talk about how I have allowed all of this to happen. What have I learned about me? I want to be as vulnerable and honest as possible.

We both move another 90 degrees. Now they are standing in the spot where I started and I in their spot. I let them explain why they did what they did. They are totally honest. With God and the Holy Spirit helping, they know exactly why they did what they did.

I move 90 degrees. I forgive them for WHY they did what they did. I may not necessarily forgive *what* they did, but I can pray that will come in time. For now, I focus on the *why*. This is pragmatic: I don't want to go through life carrying this with me. I am declaring that I want to honestly be done with it.

I move 90 degrees back to my starting position. I take back the power that I gave to them. I take back the energy that I lost. I may see a spark of Light coming from them to me or they can toss any object, ball of energy, etc. They retreat into the woods.

I can now walk into the center of the circle and cheer or cry or whatever feeling is coming up for me in this meditation. I can act out in the circle. Sometimes, rain feels good to wash and cleanse me. Sometimes I call in a deceased relative to hug me. Sometimes I just stand there and let the sunlight or the Light of unconditional love warm me. I say a prayer of thanks and when I am ready, I return to this reality.[8]

I have also taken my clients who are ready to forgive out into nature, where we draw a circle on the ground. They sit in the middle and write a list of all the things this person had done to hurt them. We build a small fire using sage inside a circle of stones. We ask God and the Holy Spirit as we burn the paper to lift the burden from my clients and we blow the smoke in the direction of the other person.

I did this recently in a state park with a client who was physically abused by his father throughout his childhood. He brought stones with him that he had collected over the years to make our circle for the fire. He picked a place in the woods where a huge tree had fallen and broken in half so it formed a huge V. We sat under the V. We prayed together and then he wrote. For a half hour he wrote. We burned the paper with the sage, letting the smoke go straight up because his father was dead.

---

[8] Adapted from a Lazaris Workshop.

Although this ritual may not necessarily turn out to be for-giveness, it does lift a lot of the pain and bring in renewed energy.

Whenever we ask God and the Holy Spirit in, there is a definite "lifting" to our experiences.

## Guided Imagery

Here are three guided imageries I use in workshops and with clients. As you will read, they are profound and power-ful. Read them one at a time when you are relaxed and have lots of time to think each one over. Then tape-record the ones you want to try in your own voice.

## Pillar of Light

Here's a short, easy guided imagery that I use sometimes to connect for a healing session or whenever I want to affirm my connection to spirit.

Visualize a huge ball of white Light way up high above you. A pillar or column comes down and enters your head, filling you with white Light. Then project it out through your chest at heart level.

If you are doing a hands-on healing, then visualize the Light coming out through your hands and forming a ball of white Light wherever there is pain in the person you are giv-ing to.

## Chakra Balancing

This guided imagery with colors is for balancing the chakras. I do it once a week and occasionally when I feel I need it. You may be sitting or lying down. Before starting any guided imagery, take two or three deep cleansing breaths. Start the inhalation from your abdomen. Inhale through your nostrils slowly. Exhale slowly through pursed lips, as though you have a straw in your mouth. Tell yourself, "Breathing in relaxation, breathing out stress." Feel your whole body relax. Do a body check. Start at your feet and slowly go up your body, asking each part to relax, including your scalp, your face and especially around your eyes. Check your throat and swallow if you need to. Now you are ready to begin.

Visualize bright red Light energy entering the base of your spine and filling your pelvis. The red energy is now flowing down through the lower half of your body, filling your legs, pouring through your ankles and into your feet, spilling out of your toes, down through the floor and into the planet. The red Light energy is taking all the negativity and toxins with it into the Earth.

There is orange Light energy flowing into you about two inches below your navel. It is filling your abdomen. Every cell, every tissue and every organ is bathed in orange Light. This orange Light is moving up through your body. Up into your lungs and now flowing into your heart. Your whole body is glowing in bright orange Light energy. And now the Light is flowing out of your chest at heart level, taking all the negativity and toxins with it.

Golden white Light energy is flowing into your body at the level of your diaphragm. It is filling your body, permeating every cell, every tissue and every organ with this beautiful, radiant Light. It cleanses and energizes every cell, every tissue and every organ, and then flows out of your chest at heart level.

Deep green healing Light energy is flowing into your heart now. It floods your heart and spills over into your chest, shoulders and arms. It moves down your whole body, healing as it flows. Every cell, every tissue and every organ is healed. The healing green Light energy is flowing down into your legs. Now it is flowing up into your throat and head, filling your neck and then your brain, your mind and your aura in healing green Light.

Deep blue Light energy is flowing into your throat. Now it is moving down into your chest and filling your heart. Your heart and your throat are connected now with blue Light, so you can say what you feel from your heart.

Indigo Light energy is flowing into your forehead now between your eyebrows. The indigo Light is filling your brain, your mind and your soul with indigo Light energy. Flowing now through your throat, into your chest and filling your heart.

Violet Light energy is spilling into the top of your head, filling your brain and your mind and your soul with spiritual energy from the Universe. The violet Light energy is flowing down through your throat and into your chest, filling your heart with infinite amounts of spiritual energy.

Breathing in relaxation through your nostrils, and blowing out stress from pursed lips. When you are ready, open your eyes.

## A Near-Death Experience

This guided imagery should be stretched over 20 minutes if you decide to tape-record it. Do the breathing described above. Then do a body check, starting at your feet and moving up your body, asking each part to relax. Give yourself at least a half hour after listening to integrate what happened.

Let's suppose you have decided to put this book down and walk outside. As you do, you walk to the street to talk to some people you know who are walking by, and as you approach them you are suddenly viewing them from above. You are looking at the tops of their heads and they are gathering around a body. You recognize it as your own. There is a car pulled over and the driver is saying to the group that he didn't see you when you stepped off the curb from behind the tree. They are all leaning over you, yelling for you to open your eyes. You move closer, trying to tell them that it is only your body on the ground. You are fine. As you grab one person's shoulder, you see your hand go right through him. You look up, trying to figure out what is going on. Way up above the roof you see this beautiful being waving to you, smiling and inviting you to join her. And as you think you want to go to her, you are face to face with her and she smiles and moves you toward an opening through this reality into a space that is dark, yet you can see. She peers in your eyes and instantly you understand that everything is all right and this is perfect.

You're moving through a huge black to gray enclosure, it is becoming lighter. There is a gentle breeze caressing you, a low sound beckoning you. She motions for you to look ahead and there is a beautiful pulsating golden white Light waiting for you to enter it. Warmth, love, compassion, joy permeate through you as you move into the Light and merge with it. You are the Light. You are huge, infinite and you have the wisdom of this Light within you.

You move through the other side of the Light into a meadow with flowers and trees containing colors you have never seen before. It's as though your entire life had been in flat black and white, and suddenly the world is 3-D color. From the other side of a stream deceased relatives and/or friends whom you remember lovingly are coming over to greet you. They surround you and circle you, smiling. No words are spoken. Communication is direct; their hearts are sending you everything they want to say directly into your heart. Your chest—at the level of your heart—feels warm and blissful and you communicate back to them by sending a heart message. Your chest feels like the Light, only it's your size now.

Suddenly, you are a small child back in the bedroom you had at the beginning of this life. Your parents are there and your sisters, brothers, aunts, uncles and cousins. Your grandparents come in and are young again. All of you are young and you relive your childhood, feeling their feelings as well as your own. You are understanding what is going on in your childhood from their hearts as well as your own.

And now you are growing up. You are 20: then 30: you are back to this present day. Back in the meadow. Everyone is smiling, kissing you or waving good-bye, letting you know heart to heart that someday you will be back, and they will be there for you, but now you must return. It is not your time. You have much to do.

And your guide, this beautiful being, is taking you back through the Light. And it feels wonderful. She letting you know It is always with you, in your heart. And you are back in the darkness, traveling, moving toward an opening that has the planet Earth way off in the distance. Earth is so beautiful. As soon as you think how beautiful it is and that you want to be back, you are. You are looking up at the faces of your neighbors who are bending over you as the paramedics are working on you. They see your eyes open and everyone is yelling and crying joyfully that you are alive.

Welcome back!

Finally, as suggested through this book, awakening and embracing our soul and spirit can be done through meditation; spiritual books and talks; or selfless service, such as volunteering at a hospital, hospice or some kind of work with the elderly. And overlapping everything else: living our lives from our hearts, living in unconditional love.

# TWELVE

# Living in Unconditional Love

E ach transformational journey is unique. There is not one ideal state of being or one destination. This process varies as each individual varies. There is, however, one ideal we all share, and that is unconditional love. Unconditional love is happy doing many things that ego is bored with. It is blatantly different from egoic love, with its desires and power plays. It leads in a different direction, toward the goodness, the value and the needs of the people around us.

Loving ourselves, we can negotiate our willingness to work with other people's moods, problems and difficult points. And by developing healthy boundaries, others can't project their unfinished business onto us in a way that could hurt. Unconditional love then allows deeper penetration through layers of ourselves. It becomes the last context we can create for ourselves before we must *finally let go and just be.*

## Letting Go—Again and Again

The action, or non-action, that experiencers describe as their NDE begins is surrender or letting go. Charles Whitfield repeats the theme of letting go when he lists the first of his three factors in transforming our attachment to our false self to living as our True Self. The type of sex described in chapter 10 begins with letting go. So does meditation, free-form prayer or any type of energy work. We let go of our egos, we stand aside and make room for God's presence.

Often in our transformational journey, when we have stood on the threshold of each new level, surrendering or letting go was the key that allowed us to move forward. Surrendering takes new courage every time, but it gets us out of our own way, and we grow.

What is required of us to move forward from the threshold and into the Light-filled level of God's unconditional love is to let go. Healing began for many of us in our spiritual awakenings, as we realized we no longer needed to be victims because there was no longer any value in holding onto our pain. So we let it go. This theme, subtle as it may have once been, becomes a current flowing through the changes that we make. We let go of our past and live in the present moment.

When I am whole, when I am living as my True Self, standing in the Light of my own soul, I can help the people I love by being present with them and loving them unconditionally. But I can't fix anyone. I surrendered my ego's need to control this reality I share with my loved ones and moved into the larger Reality, where my inner life and the Light of unconditional love work together. As I moved into balance, my relationships moved into balance.

As I give everyone around me the space to be who they are, which is also unconditional love, I'm giving myself the same space. One of the rules of the Universe becomes so obvious: We treat others as we want to be treated and then everything we give out comes back.

## Unconditional Love

Love is different from what I had once believed before my awakening. It is different from what my ego wanted, different from the Hollywood fantasies of inflated enchantment. Love turns out to be real. It turns out to be what I am, rather than what my ego demands.

Love is the power within our core that affirms and values another person rather than the ideal our egos would like them to be, the projection that flows from our false self. Love is the inner God who opens our blind eyes to the beauty, value and quality of the other person. Love causes us to value that person as a total, individual self, and this means that we accept the negative side as well as the positive, the imperfections as well as the admirable qualities. When one truly loves the human being rather than the projection, one loves and accepts the other person's totality.[1]

God held me in my life review, and I experienced the pain and the love I had been responsible for in all my relationships for 32 years. Since then, in uncovering and working to heal my True Self I have experientially realized that *my True Self is unconditional love* already there waiting to just be. All I have to do is be authentically who I am. I *am* unconditional love at my core.[2] My True Self is a mirror of God's unconditional love. Therefore, when the little mirror hooks up with the big one, unlimited amounts of unconditional love result, which also allows deeper and deeper penetration through these layers of questions I cannot yet answer. Unconditional love becomes the last context we can create for ourselves before we must finally let go and just be.

The doorway that once opened in this reality and let me go through to the bigger Reality we call death has opened again, not just in meditation, but here and now. It feels like

---

[1] Johnson, *We: Understanding the Psychology of Romantic Love.*
[2] Harris, 1990; Whitfield, 1991.

this: Every time I ask for help with a relationship, almost immediately help happens in ways I could have never predicted. This help is always softer and more loving than I could have imagined, and comes with integrity and tenderness—there are no painful confrontations except an occasional loving confrontation where I am flooded with knowledge about myself, the other person or the relationship. It appears to me as though I am back in my life review. I can feel what the other is feeling. I can see the bigger picture. The Reality of the other side is this Reality, too. And I can trust the Divine Energy to work in others as it is working in me.

Sometimes what I learn about the other person is not what I had wanted that person to be. However, unconditional love remains firm. Real love begins only when one person comes to know another for who that person *really is* as a human being. We get closer to the whole picture, the truth of who another is and *who we are.*

This reality now is interchangeable with my original life review. I am aware of God's presence and I am aware that I have the choice of choosing pain or choosing love, choosing projection or expanding and becoming my potential. We know that each one of us is a unique reflection of God. *Not to develop to our potential is to deny God another facet of Its being.*

Time and space are still different from the way they were before my awakening. Each day, each new experience has the quality of the bubbles in my life review. I move from bubble to bubble, co-creating my life with God's energy of unconditional love. And the Light outshines the darkness.

I am learning to let go every moment and accept all of my experience—courage and fear, celebration and pain, expansiveness and limitation. Staying tough and tender at the same time, this strength is coming from my core or Child Within. Every one of us who struggles to learn unconditional love is giving birth to that child. The faint inner voice that awakened in our spiritual experience is now the child we have searched for, given birth to and now embrace, bonding in unconditional love.

And so it is at this level of human consciousness. We passed through this reality into the Reality of the bigger consciousness, each in our own way, through nearly dying, meditation, asking in prayer, bottoming out, giving birth, spontaneously, in a dream, and so on and so on. We are removed from our limited existence and come face to face with the Universe. Then we are suddenly back here, and some like me will struggle with this new awareness, and then finally learn to let go and let God. *It is not that we were chosen—it is that we chose God.* We opened to God. Then we choose to invite unconditional love, the action of Divine Energy, into our lives. We live our own potential. And it hits us one day, probably the same day we notice it is the same on both sides of Reality.

*We're all inside God, and God is making love through us!*

## God's Will

When all five billion of us live life sharing unconditional love, we may become the synergy of God. We take our conflicting currents and turn them into harmony. We transcend right and wrong, Yin and Yang, and unite our opposites. We heal the split and embrace something new, something born from balance. This is what the mystery of God may be. It is not an easy task, but ultimately it is the one we may have been given. God's will is our highest human potential, shared.

# Appendix I

## The Child Within

In his national bestseller *Healing the Child Within,* Charles L. Whitfield, M.D., describes the *false self* or *negative ego.* Our false self takes over when we are mistreated or abused as children. Our True Self or Child Within (our core) goes into hiding and lets our false self run our lives for protection. For those of us who can remember now being confronted as children with trauma, neglect, shame and/or abuse (see table 2), that treatment sent our child into hiding at an early age. We learned not to be in touch with the Child part of ourselves. Our survival depended upon developing a false self, and because we needed to survive, we often left the Child hidden as we moved into the adult world. The system worked when we were kids and needed to hide. The trouble is that now our Child has been so deeply buried that we forgot it, and our false self believes that it is the totality of who we are. *This false self dies when our body dies. For those of us who have had spiritual awakening experiences—our ego/false self started to die or died.* (Is it any wonder some of us feel confused when we are back here again?)

---

### Table 1

### Some Characteristics of Our Core or Child Within

| | |
|---|---|
| Authentic self | Non-defensive, though may at times use ego defenses |
| True Self | Connected to Higher Power |
| Genuine | Open to unconscious |
| Spontaneous | Remembers our Oneness |
| Expansive, loving | Free to grow |
| Giving, communicating | Private self |
| Accepting of self and others | Our Core |
| Compassionate | Our Heart |
| Loves unconditionally | Our Soul |
| Feels feelings, including appropriate, spontaneous current anger | Self-indulgent Simplifies |
| Assertive | Wants to be real, connect experience, create and love |
| Intuitive | Earthy |
| Inner Child; ability to be child-like | Trusting Enjoys being nurtured |
| Needs to play and have fun | Surrenders |
| Vulnerable | Innocent |
| Powerful in true sense | |

*Adapted from Whitfield, 1987*

---

Within the term *Child Within* is the recognition that inside each of us, there is a child. This concept is major. Historically, this Child has been given many names. Alice Miller, in her work on child abuse, calls it the "True Self"; Carl Jung refers to it as the "Divine Child"; others call it the "Magical Child"; and those who work in the Adult Child field often refer to this child as the "Inner Child" or the "Child Within." *This is our Real Self—who we really are. It is also the part of us that con-*

*tinues existing after we die. We might even say our Child Within is the part of us that is a reflection of God.*

## Defining Abuse or Trauma

Table 2 lists terms for mental, emotional and spiritual trauma that may be experienced by children and adults. Can you identify with any of these terms? If you can—as I can—then what I am describing in this section will make some sense.

Even if you grew up in a healthy environment—if you are now in a close relationship with someone who didn't, who is addicted, disordered or otherwise dysfunctional, you very likely have lost your True Self in that relationship or in your life. Our spiritual awakenings then remind us of who we really are.

---

### Table 2

---

### Some Terms for Mental, Emotional and Spiritual Trauma that May Be Experienced by Children and Adults

Abandonment
Neglect
Abuse:
  Physical—spanking, torture, sexual, etc.
  Mental—covert sexual (see below)
  Emotional (see below)
  Spiritual (see below)

| | |
|---|---|
| Shaming | Limiting |
| Humiliating | Withdrawing |
| Degrading | Withholding love |
| Inflicting guilt | Not taking seriously |
| Criticizing | Discrediting |
| Disgracing | Misleading |
| Joking about | Disapproving |
| Laughing at | Making light of or minimizing |
| Teasing | your feelings, wants or needs |
| Manipulating | Breaking promises |
| Deceiving | Raising hopes falsely |
| Tricking | Responding inconsistently or |
| Betraying | arbitrarily |
| Hurting | Making vague demands |

Being Cruel
Belittling
Intimidating
Patronizing
Threatening
Inflicting fear
Overpowering or bullying
Controlling

Stifling
Saying "You shouldn't feel
   such & such," e.g., anger
Saying, "If only you were better
   or different," or "You should
   be better or different"

# Appendix II

## Spiritual Emergence Network

The Spiritual Emergence Network (SEN) is a volunteer organization operating mainly by telephone for those having a spiritual awakening and needing a compassionate listener. The volunteer will then attempt to find a referral that is right for the caller's needs. From a variety of backgrounds—mental health, holistic health, teaching, art in various media, business—the volunteers all share a commitment to their own spiritual path and to supporting the spiritual process in others. Most have also experienced a critical and frightening period in their spiritual emergence and can truthfully say to the caller, "I know just about what you are going through. I've been there." There are presently about 20 volunteers. Twelve of them answer the telephone; the rest are involved in researching answers for callers and writing letters. Telephone coverage averages between 30 and 35 hours a week. The referral network is composed of psychiatrists and psychologists, shamans, breath workers, clergy and "listeners" from spiritual retreat centers to hospitals. Services are free to callers. SEN membership provides their necessary income. Their phone number is 408-464-8261; or you may write to them at 603 Mission St., Santa Cruz, CA 95060-3653.

## Kundalini Research Network

The Kundalini Research Network (KRN) is a group of individuals dedicated to the research of the experience of energy/consciousness known as Kundalini in the ancient Indian tradition, and recognized cross-culturally in every esoteric and mystical tradition. Their goal is to support one another in their efforts to bring the existence of the phenomenon of Kundalini and the conditions that often occur with its arousal to the attention of the Western world, especially the scientific and medical communities, therapists and health care professionals, and people undergoing Kundalini experiences. Their yearly research conferences include a mixture of theoretical, clinical and experiential processes.

If you would like to become a member of the Kundalini Research Network, write to: KRN, RR #5, Flesherton, Ontario, Canada NOC 1EO. Yvonne Kason, M.D., Leaside Health Center, 795 Eglinton Ave. East, Toronto, Ontario, Canada M4G 4E4.

## The International Association of Near-Death Studies

The International Association of Near-Death Studies (IANDS) is the only organization in the world devoted to the study of near-death experiences. It is an information center for those who have had an NDE or are interested researchers. IANDS facilitates support and information services to the experiencer, his or her family, and helping professionals who have special needs in coping with the aftereffects of an NDE. IANDS encourages and helps facilitate research and academic interest. *The Journal of Near-Death Studies* is published quarterly by IANDS and is the only scholarly journal in the field. *Vital Signs* is the quarterly newsletter (available to members) that contains experience accounts, commentaries and association news.

The address is IANDS, P.O. Box 502, East Windsor Hill, CT 06028.

The phone number is 203-528-5144.

The address for the research division and the editorial address for the journal: Bruce Greyson, M.D., Department of Psychiatry, University of Connecticut Health Center, Farmington CT 06030-6410.

# Bibliography

Anand, M. *The Art of Sexual Ecstasy*. Los Angeles, California: Tarcher, 1989.

Bentov, I. *Stalking the Wild Pendulum: On the Mechanics of Consciousness*. Rochester, Vermont: Inner Traditions, 1977.

Bentov, I., with M. Bentov. *A Cosmic Book on the Mechanics of Creation*. New York: E. P. Dutton, 1982.

*A Course in Miracles*. Tiburon, California: Foundation for Inner Peace, 1975.

Dossey, L. *Beyond Illness*. Boulder, Colorado: Shambala, 1984.

———. *Recovering the Soul*. New York: Bantam, 1989.

———. *Space, Time and Machine*. Boulder, Colorado: Shambala, 1982.

Ferguson, M. *The Aquarian Conspiracy*. Los Angeles, California: J. P. Tarcher, 1980.

Gordon, R. *Your Healing Hands*. Santa Cruz, California: Unity Press, 1979.

Greenwell, B. *Energies of Transformation: A Guide to the Kundalini Process*. Cupertino, California: Shakti River Press/Transpersonal Learning Services, 1990.

Greyson, B. "Increase in Psychic Phenomena Following Near-Death Experiences." *Theta* 11 (1983): 26-29.

——. "Near-Death Experiences and the Physio-Kundalini Syndrome." *Journal of Religion & Health* 32, no. 4 (winter 1993): 277-289.

——. "Physio-Kundalini Syndrome and Mental Illness." *Journal of Transpersonal Psychology* 25, no. 1 (1993): 43-57.

——. Scientific commentary in B. Harris and L. Bascom *Full Circle: The Near-Death Experience and Beyond.* New York: Pocket Books, 1990.

Greyson, B. and B. Harris. "Clinical Approaches to the NDEr." *Journal of Near-Death Studies* 6, no. 1 (fall 1987): 41-52.

Greyson, B. and B. Harris, ed. "Counseling the Near-Death Experiencers." Grof & Grof, eds. *Spiritual Emergency: When Personal Transformation Becomes a Crisis.* Los Angeles, California: J.P. Tarcher, 1989: 199-210.

Hardt, J. "Kundalini and Biofeedback." Paper presented to the First International Conference on Energies of Transformation, Asilomar, CA, 1990.

Harris, B. "Kundalini and Healing in the West." *Journal of Near-Death Studies* 13, no. 2 (winter 1994): 75-79.

Harris, B. and L. Bascom. *Full Circle: The Near-Death Experience and Beyond.* New York: Pocket Books, 1990.

Henderson, I. *The Lover Within.* Barrytown, New York: Station Hill, 1986.

Iasos. *Angelic Music* (Compact Disc and Cassette). Sausalito, California: Inter-dimensional Music.

Johnson, R. *We: Understanding the Psychology of Romantic Love.* San Francisco, California: Harper and Row, 1983.

Karagulla, S. *Breakthrough to Creativity.* Marina Del Rey, California: DeVorss & Co.,1967.

Keen, S. *The Passionate Life.* San Francisco, California: Harper and Row, 1983.

Keyes, K. *Handbook to Higher Consciousness.* Marina Del Rey, California: Living Love Center, 1975.

Kohr, R. "Near-Death Experience and Its Relationship to Psi and Various Altered States." *Theta* 10 (1982): 50-53.

——. "A Survey of Psi Experiences among Members of a Special Population." *Journal of the American Society for Psychical Research* 74 (1980): 395-411.

Krishna, G. *Kundalini: The Evolutionary Energy in Man.* Berkeley,

California: Shambhala, 1971.

Kunz, D. *Spiritual Aspects of the Healing Arts*. Wheaton, Illinois: Theosophical Publishing House, 1985.

LaBerge, S. *Lucid Dreaming*. Los Angeles, California: J. P. Tarcher, 1985.

LaBerge, S. and H. Rheingold. *Exploring the World of Lucid Dreaming*. New York: Ballantine, 1990.

Lazaris Workshops. Palm Beach, Florida: Concept Synergy.

Maslow, A. *The Farther Reaches of Human Nature*. New York: Penguin, 1971.

May, G. *The Awakened Heart*. San Francisco, California: Harper San Francisco, 1991.

Moss, R. *The Black Butterfly*. Millbrae, California: Celestial Arts, 1986.

—— *The I That Is We*. Millbrae, California: Celestial Arts, 1988.

Newsome, R.D. "Ego, Moral Faith Development in Near-Death Experiencers: Three Case Studies." *Journal of Near-Death Studies* 7, no. 2 (winter 1988): 73-105.

Nouwen, H. J. *Life of the Beloved*. New York: Crossroads, 1993.

Paine-Gernee, K. and T. Hunt. *Emotional Healing*. New York: Warner Books, 1990.

Pearce, J. *Magical Child Matures*. New York: E.P. Dutton, Inc., 1985.

Powell, J. *Unconditional Love*. Allen, Texas: Arugus Communications 1978.

Ring, K. *Heading Toward Omega*. New York: Morrow, 1984.

——. *The Omega Project*. New York: Morrow, 1993.

Ring, K. and C. Rosing. "The Omega Project." *The Journal of Near-Death Studies* 8, no. 4 (1990): 211-239.

St. John, Gloria. *The Way Home: A Journey Throughout the Chakras*. Unpublished, from a workshop at KRN Conference, June, 1992. 1400 Shattuck, Berkeley, Suite 7-126, CA 94709.

Sannella, L. *Kundalini: Psychosis or Transcendence*. Lower Lake, California: Integral Publishing, 1987.

Shallis, M. *The Electric Connection: Its Effects on Mind and Body*. New York: New Amsterdam, 1989.

Siegel, B. *Love, Medicine and Miracles*. New York: Harper and Row, 1986.

Silver, N. "The Cosmic Pulse: Where Sex and Spirit Meet." *Gnosis Journal* no.17 (fall 1990): 20–25.

Small, J. *Awakening in Time*. New York: Bantam, 1991.

——. U.S. Journal Workshop. Baltimore, Maryland, 1991.

Stubbs, K. *Sacred Orgasms*. Larkspur, California: Secret Garden Publishing, 1992.

Thompson, K. "The Future of the Body." *Yoga Journal*, 86 (1989): 38-45.

Travell, J. and D. Simons. *Myofascial Pain and Dysfunction: The Trigger Point Manual*. Baltimore, Maryland: Williams and Wilkins, 1993.

Von Urban, R. *Sex Perfection and Marital Happiness*. New York: Dial Press, 1949.

Walsh, R. "The Transpersonal Movement: A History and State of the Art." *Revisions Journal* 16, no. 3 (winter 1994): 115-122.

Walsh, R. and F. Vaughn, eds. *Beyond Ego*. Los Angeles, California: J. P. Tarcher, 1980.

——. *Paths Beyond Ego*. Los Angeles, California: J. P. Tarcher 1993.

Watts, A. *Nature, Man and Woman*. New York: Vintage Books, 1970.

Weil, A. *Natural Health, Natural Medicine*. New York: Houghton Mifflin Co., 1990.

——. *The Natural Mind*. New York: Houghton Mifflin Co., 1972.

Welwood, J., ed. *Awakening the Heart*. Boulder Colorado: Shambhala, New Science Library, 1983.

Welwood, J. "The Healing Power of Unconditional Presence." *Quest* 5, no. 4 (winter 1992): 35-40.

Whitfield, C. *Boundaries and Relationships*. Deerfield Beach, Florida: Health Communications, Inc., 1993.

——. *Co-dependence: Healing the Human Condition*. Deerfield Beach, Florida: Health Communications, Inc., 1991.

——. *A Gift to Myself*. Deerfield Beach, Florida: Health Communications, Inc., 1991.

——. *Healing the Child Within*. Deerfield Beach, Florida: Health Communications, Inc., 1987.

——. *Memory and Abuse*. Deerfield Beach, Florida: Health Communications, Inc., 1995.

——. *My Recovery Plan* (booklets for each of the three stages of recovery). Deerfield Beach, Florida: Health Communications, 1992-93.

——. *Spirituality in Recovery*. Pre-print available by calling 1-800-770-8811.

Wong, B.P. and J. McKeen. *A Manual for Life*. Unpublished, 1990.

——. "Transpersonal Experience Through Body Approaches." *Transpersonal Psychotherapy*. S. Boorstein ed. Palo Alto,

California: Science and Behavior Press, 1980.

Zukav, G. *The Dancing Wu Li Masters*. New York: Quill, 1979.

——. *Seat of the Soul*. New York: Simon and Schuster, 1989.

# Index

181

# About the Author

Barbara Harris Whitfield is a respiratory and massage therapist who works with people who are seeking to integrate and expand their spiritual experiences. She also specializes in helping people who were wounded from childhood trauma.

In 1975, after spinal surgery, Barbara had two profound near-death experiences. Wanting answers to what had happened and somehow feeling a "sense of mission," she went back to school to pursue a health care career. She graduated as a respiratory therapist and practiced in hospital critical care units, often hearing profound descriptions of near-death experiences from her patients. After meeting University of Connecticut psychology professor Kenneth Ring and working with him toward an understanding of this phenomenon, she became a prime subject in his second book *Heading Toward Omega: In Search of the Meaning of the NDE.* She then founded and facilitated several support groups in Florida for NDErs (near-death experiencers). She continued facilitating support groups in Connecticut during her six years of research assisting psychiatry professor Bruce Greyson at the University of Connecticut Medical School. This research was dedicated to the aftereffects of near-death experiences and psychospiritual openings in general. At this time she continued her research on the bioenergetic changes of spiritual opening by pursuing an education as a certified massage therapist. Dr. Greyson and Ms. Whitfield co-authored a groundbreaking article for the *Journal of Near-Death Studies,* "Clinical Approaches to the NDEr" and this has been reprinted in her first book *Full Circle: The Near-Death Experience and Beyond.* She has presented workshops and lectures for hospices, hospitals, massage therapy schools and universities throughout the United States and Canada on this research. She is presently on the faculty of Rutgers University's Summer School of Alcohol and Drug Studies where she teaches classes on "Spiritual Awakenings: When the 12th Step Happens First" and "Relationships in Advanced Recovery: A New Intimacy."

Ms. Whitfield is in private practice in Baltimore and Atlanta and also presents workshops nationally. These workshops break new ground, helping attendees to expand their beliefs so they can bring their Higher Nature into everyday life. She offers a new paradigm in health care, emerging as a compliment to traditional Western psychology and medicine. This paradigm incorporates a variety of body-based and psychological therapies that validate the role of the True Self in health and wholeness. She also presents workshops specifically for nursing groups, massage therapists, mental health workers and other helping professionals.

To be on her mailing list for lectures and workshops in your area, or if you would like to sponsor a workshop in your area, please send a self–addressed stamped envelope to: Whitfield Workshops, P.O. Box 5088, Hollywood, FL 33083-5088.